Complete Horoscope

Libra 2023

Monthly astrological forecasts for 2023

TATIANA BORSCH

Translated from Russian by Sonja Swenson
Translation copyright © Coinflow Limited, Cyprus
AstraArt Books is an imprint of Coinflow limited, Cyprus
Published by Coinflow Limited, Cyprus
For queries please contact: tatianaborsch@yahoo.com

ISBN978-9925-609-07-9(paperback)
ISBN 978-9925-609-08-6(ebook)

Contents

2023 – The Great Transition Continues

In previous forecasts, I have described the unique transition period in which the world finds itself.

I will summarize for those who have not read my predictions for 2020, 2021, and 2022.

We have entered a period of changes, and the world has come to a fateful point, where everything that seemed constant and unshakable no longer is. If that is the case, then what awaits us?

From an astrological perspective, 2020, 2021, and 2022 are extensions of one long period, and cannot be divided. This is a time of major changes in every nation, home, and individual.

There is no comparison for this period in modern history. In fact, humanity has not lived through a period quite like this for a very long time.

The astrological explanation for this is that we are living through a grandiose shift in eras. The Age of Pisces, which lasted for 2,160 years, is transitioning into the Age of Aquarius.

2023 fits naturally into this complex sequence. This is an important and critical watershed.

During the first half of 2023, we see a natural continuation of a very complicated period that began in 2022. The confrontation between East and West will continue in Ukraine, as will rivalry between the United States and China, along with financial and economic crises that have beset the entire world.

As of June 2022, when this forecast is being written, I can predict that in the fall of 2022, that is in October and November, the conflict between Russia and the West in Ukraine will reach a new level. Russia's advancements will force the West, including the United States, to take on a more active role in the face of the invasion in Ukraine, as the entire world risks being dragged into a new war.

The stars predict that the war in Ukraine may come to an end in January-February 2023. Ukraine will be divided into two zones of influence, with much of its territory falling under Russia's shadow. Volodymyr Zelenskyy will lose his grip on power and may flee the country, and Ukrainian leadership will be replaced. Peace initiatives that might otherwise be capable of changing this tragic situation will constantly be thwarted. In January 2023, aggressive Mars will no longer be in retrograde, and by February, there will be a light at the end of the tunnel. Initially, it will be just a flicker, but it is certainly better than nothing.

Gradually, the countries involved in this conflict will come to realize that they need to hold constructive negotiations in order to meet all of society's healthy demands and trends. These talks will not be swift, and they will probably only bear fruit in the second half of 2023.

Overall, despite Ukraine's valiant efforts both militarily and politically, along with support from the West, Russia will prevail, militarily, geopolitically, and ideologically.

This will seriously alter the geopolitical landscape on the global stage. In time, Asia and Russia will dominate the world's economy. The events of this year are just one more step in the transition as global influence shifts eastward. Tensions between the United States and Asian countries will only heat up.

In late 2022 and early 2023, many countries' economies will descend into chaos, and a general financial crisis will drag down banks, companies, and the entire planet's population.

In many Western countries, antiwar sentiment will be palpable, and there may be demonstrations, protests, and other expressions of dissatisfaction with governments.

In Russia, the fall of 2022 and first half of 2023 will see widespread changes in the structures of power. Western sanctions will lead to serious economic losses, forcing Russia to find a way to survive in the face of Western and American economic aggression.

The worst economic crisis will take place in the United States. The fall of 2022 and during the first half of 2023 may be the worst period it has faced in recent memory. There may be serious confrontations between political parties, which might throw American society as a whole off balance. During the fall of 2022 and first half of 2023, President Biden will experience serious difficulties. The stars predict he will face worsening health, along with serious destabilization of the entire American financial system. (A president's horoscope is responsible for much of what will happen to his or her country). During the same period, Bident's great foe, former President Trump, is expected to become much more active and powerful.

European countries will not be spared, either. In France, opposition to President Macron's policies will grow and Macron will lose some of his influence.

In Germany, Chancellor Olaf Scholz will become more aggressive during the fall. Despite his outward calm, he may turn out to be an active supporter of Western support for Ukraine. This will lead to a backlash in German society, and by May 2023, Scholz will be in a much weaker position than he is today.

From November 2022 to May 2023, the United Kingdom may see changes in leadership. This will be a period full of obstacles, including serious financial difficulties, demonstrations by those who disagree with the political power structure, and a trend of separatism in the various regions. In June-July, things will calm down significantly, and the British financial and political system will manage to recover.

The second half of May will also be a time of challenges. Jupiter will square Pluto during this time, with support from aggressive Mars. We can expect cataclysms and changes in many countries' governments here. Serious acts of terrorism cannot be ruled out, either.

During the second half of 2023, Jupiter will transition from the bellicose sign of Aries into the more peaceful sign of Taurus, and its favorable aspect with Saturn in June gives reason to hope that things are likely to improve.

That process will not be overnight, however. We see evidence of that in Uranus, which will be in the sign of Taurus, at the same degrees as during the period of World War II. Taurus symbolizes life and all its peaceful manifestations, while Uranus is the symbol of renewal through destruction. That portends a break with old structures, which may unleash war, death, and political and economic clashes.

All of these painful processes will eventually lead to the birth of a new, modern world, but that will not be completed until after 2025.

Looking at the future, I predict that in late 2022, and early 2023, economic, political, and social, as well as personal crises will reach a peak. Remember, we are blessed to live in an era of great change, and historical events certainly do leave their mark on our personal lives.

I also predict that during the second half of 2023, we will reach the halfway point on this long and winding road, and this may be the most complicated part of that trajectory. After this point, people will begin looking for a way to resolve the world's most pressing problems, and the light at the end of the tunnel may start to glimmer a bit brighter. Of course, this is inevitable, but step by step, people will start to tackle the many challenges we face. This is a gradual, sometimes painful process. But there is hope that Fate will have less unpleasant surprises in store for us and life will start running a bit more smoothly. It will never go back to exactly the way it was, but as this period draws to a close, we will see that in one way or another, all of these changes are for the best.

Money

We may face a global banking system crisis, which is likely to happen in November-December 2022. I believe it would be wiser to hold your money in something tangible, like real estate, land, or gold, than in the banking system or simply on paper. Purchasing power may experience a serious decline.

Health

Health-wise, anyone with thyroid problems or cardiovascular disease or any illnesses involving the blood vessels of the brain should be particularly cautious. We see this as Uranus transits into Taurus.

Pluto is still in Capricorn, which exacerbates musculoskeletal and bone disorders. Teeth are also in Pluto's crosshairs, so it is best to treat them quickly!

Cancer cases may rise, so do not hesitate to visit the doctor quickly, as cancer is only treatable in the early stages.

In 2023, Saturn is transiting into Pisces – this may lead to problems for those with various types of diabetes or problems involving the legs.

During the spring and fall of 2023, more outbreaks of unknown diseases and viruses are possible.

Nature

In 2023, various natural anomalies that the world has been struggling with may continue. Jupiter in Aries might cause fires, which will be a destabilizing factor during the winter and spring of 2023.

However, in early May, when Jupiter transitions into Taurus, we can expect to see significant improvements in agriculture. Harvests will be more abundant, which, in many countries, will mean a way out of the food crisis. Many countries will also be able to invest more in agriculture production and processing, which will only revive small towns and villages.

Fashion

Jupiter will be in Aries during the first half of 2023, and this promises all shades of red, which will be on models everywhere during this period. Many people will instinctively be drawn to red, as Aries's energy simply hangs in the air. Military-inspired dress may also be on the runways.

During the second half of 2023, Jupiter will transition into Taurus, which is primarily green in color. This is a great color, as it symbolizes growth and rebirth. Taurus's second color is pink, which symbolizes romanticism, softness, love for sensual pleasures and enjoyment. The fashion world may respond in kind with light, floaty fabrics and perhaps a new focus on femininity.

Have a wonderful year! Don't be afraid of crises, as they bring with them new opportunities!

Always,

Tatiana Borsch

2023 Overview for Libra

Do what you must, and the rest will fall into place – that is your motto all year long. By following it, you will achieve your goals and confirm your own rules to the game of life.

Work. This year, you will have to resolve a series of important and difficult tasks. From January to May, business owners and managers will have to grapple with problems that arose in 2022. First of all, that involves your relationship with business partners in other cities or abroad, which may have reached a critical phase in the recent past. You will put an end to this drama at some point from January to March, at which point tempers will cool.

In order to smooth over delicate issues, you may have to turn to an ally or intermediary – their influence will significantly improve things, but they are unlikely to solve this for you. During the first half of the yar, you can expect new business partners with excellent opportunities, which will give your business the impetus it needs to achieve new development and progress.

In May, Jupiter will shift, and you will see a new chapter in your life. Many Libras will think about expanding their business and be considering new locations and spaces that would be most favorable to them.

Overall, things are going according to plan, but in October and November, you will have to deal with a serious lack of funds. Perhaps your grandiose projects require a lot more money than you initially planned, and you will not manage to resolve this quandary until 2024.

Your relationship with colleagues and subordinates will require another kind of attention all year long. You may have to start with a clean slate, and that is exactly what severe Saturn, which has been in the sector of the sky responsible for work, is urging you to do.

Those with legal trouble will manage to overcome this challenge favorably during the first half of the year with the help of knowledgeable attorneys and influential people in your corner.

Employees will not see any major gains this year. During the second half of the year, you will have to think about whether you want a new job, but that will not transpire until 2024. Many will decide to open their own business during the second half of the year and make initial steps in that direction.

Money. Financially, you would be wise to prepare for the unexpected, both good and bad. The end of February will be kind to you, as will March and July. You will overcome most of your troubles in the fall, especially November, when financial issues will cause you a lot of headaches and lead to misunderstandings with your business partners or loved ones.

Love and family . Your personal life will be rich, romantic, and exciting. Single people will meet someone intriguing and this time, things look very serious. A long-term, sexy romance or a happy marriage – what could be better?

During the second half of 2023, you can expect large-scale household tasks on the agenda. You may be purchasing a new home, summer home, carrying out repairs, or other related activities. A partner who is doing well may pay an important role in all of this.

You can expect some arguments over money, and when you work on home improvements in the fall, conflict is also likely, especially in late October and November. However, by the holidays, everything will be smoothed over, and you will see that you did everything right.

Health. In 2023, you are less energetic than you could be, so take care of yourself however you need. During the second half of the year, you may tend to gain weight, so think about following a balanced diet right away and remember the importance of exercise and physical activities.

January

New York Time			London Time		
Calendar Day	Lunar Day	Lunar Day Start Time	Calendar Day	Lunar Day	Lunar Day Start Time
01/01/2023	11	12:58 PM	01/01/2023	10	12:31 PM
02/01/2023	12	1:32 PM	02/01/2023	11	12:56 PM
03/01/2023	13	2:10 PM	03/01/2023	12	1:27 PM
04/01/2023	14	2:53 PM	04/01/2023	13	2:05 PM
05/01/2023	15	3:42 PM	05/01/2023	14	2:51 PM
06/01/2023	16	4:36 PM	06/01/2023	15	3:45 PM
07/01/2023	17	5:32 PM	07/01/2023	16	4:45 PM
08/01/2023	18	6:31 PM	08/01/2023	17	5:50 PM
09/01/2023	19	7:30 PM	09/01/2023	18	6:56 PM
10/01/2023	20	8:29 PM	10/01/2023	19	8:04 PM
11/01/2023	21	9:28 PM	11/01/2023	20	9:11 PM
12/01/2023	22	10:28 PM	12/01/2023	21	10:19 PM
13/01/2023	23	11:29 PM	13/01/2023	22	11:28 PM
15/01/2023	24	12:32 AM	15/01/2023	23	12:40 AM
16/01/2023	25	1:38 AM	16/01/2023	24	1:54 AM
17/01/2023	26	2:47 AM	17/01/2023	25	3:11 AM
18/01/2023	27	3:56 AM	18/01/2023	26	4:28 AM
19/01/2023	28	5:05 AM	19/01/2023	27	5:42 AM
20/01/2023	29	6:08 AM	20/01/2023	28	6:46 AM
21/01/2023	30	7:02 AM	21/01/2023	29	7:38 AM
21/01/2023	1	3:55 PM	21/01/2023	1	8:55 PM
22/01/2023	2	7:49 AM	22/01/2023	2	8:17 AM
23/01/2023	3	8:28 AM	23/01/2023	3	8:48 AM
24/01/2023	4	9:01 AM	24/01/2023	4	9:13 AM
25/01/2023	5	9:32 AM	25/01/2023	5	9:34 AM
26/01/2023	6	10:01 AM	26/01/2023	6	9:54 AM
27/01/2023	7	10:30 AM	27/01/2023	7	10:14 AM
28/01/2023	8	11:00 AM	28/01/2023	8	10:35 AM
29/01/2023	9	11:33 AM	29/01/2023	9	11:00 AM
30/01/2023	10	12:10 PM	30/01/2023	10	11:29 AM
31/01/2023	11	12:52 PM	31/01/2023	11	12:04 PM

You can find the description of each lunar day in the chapter "A Guide to The Moon Cycle and Lunar Days"

You've just survived some difficult days, but that is all coming to an end. It should be smooth sailing from here on out, and things will be much more predictable, too. But don't let your guard down – there are still a lot of risks out there!

Work. Busy entrepreneurs and managers at every level will spend a significant part of January smoothing over relationships with partners from other cities or abroad. This will not be an easy task after everything that happened during the spring, summer, fall, and winter of 2022. However, nothing lasts forever, and now is the time to make those issues a thing of the past.

In January, you will be making important streps toward reconciliation, and, though there may be some loose ends to tie up, any progress is better than none. You might have strong allies who put their best foot forward helping you and your opponents reach an understanding. Those grappling with thorny legal issues over land or other real estate might also count on a satisfying compromise.

The first 20 days of January are likely a time for laying the groundwork, while the last 10 days, you might be able to turn all that work into positive results.

Any business travel planned in January might turn out to be very successful, though the stars recommend being careful when it comes to following any administrative laws to the letter and keeping an eye on your documents.

Money. January is a neutral month for your finances. Rather than your own sources of income, you can count on support from a loved one or family member. Business is suddenly booming for your spouse or life partner, and the whole family is reaping the benefits.

Love and family. If you are mostly focused on your personal life, here, you can count on resolving longstanding problems. Most likely, it involves misunderstandings with relatives who live in other cities or abroad. In the last 10 days of the month, you can count on a favorable resolution to some tricky problems.

Those whose marriages are on the rocks will reach an agreement on real estate, which has been a sticking point for some time, now. Your relationship with your children will soften as you reach greater understanding, and this positive trend will continue into February.

Those who are single or have been disappointed by their personal life can count on meeting someone new in late January or February. In many cases, it will be a fateful meeting.

Health. In January, you are feeling full of energy, but the stars still recommend being careful when traveling and driving. The riskiest time is the first 20 days of the month. If you are planning any trips abroad during this time, plan everything to a T and do not ignore foreign laws.

February

New York Time				London Time		
Calendar Day	Lunar Day	Lunar Day Start Time		Calendar Day	Lunar Day	Lunar Day Start Time
01/02/2023	12	1:38 PM		01/02/2023	12	12:48 PM
02/02/2023	13	2:30 PM		02/02/2023	13	1:39 PM
03/02/2023	14	3:26 PM		03/02/2023	14	2:37 PM
04/02/2023	15	4:24 PM		04/02/2023	15	3:41 PM
05/02/2023	16	5:23 PM		05/02/2023	16	4:47 PM
06/02/2023	17	6:22 PM		06/02/2023	17	5:54 PM
07/02/2023	18	7:22 PM		07/02/2023	18	7:02 PM
08/02/2023	19	8:22 PM		08/02/2023	19	8:10 PM
09/02/2023	20	9:22 PM		09/02/2023	20	9:19 PM
10/02/2023	21	10:24 PM		10/02/2023	21	10:28 PM
11/02/2023	22	11:27 PM		11/02/2023	22	11:40 PM
13/02/2023	23	12:33 AM		13/02/2023	23	12:54 AM
14/02/2023	24	1:40 AM		14/02/2023	24	2:09 AM
15/02/2023	25	2:46 AM		15/02/2023	25	3:22 AM
16/02/2023	26	3:50 AM		16/02/2023	26	4:28 AM
17/02/2023	27	4:47 AM		17/02/2023	27	5:24 AM
18/02/2023	28	5:36 AM		18/02/2023	28	6:09 AM
19/02/2023	29	6:19 AM		19/02/2023	29	6:44 AM
20/02/2023	1	2:09 AM		20/02/2023	1	7:09 AM
20/02/2023	2	6:55 AM		20/02/2023	2	7:11 AM
21/02/2023	3	7:28 AM		21/02/2023	3	7:35 AM
22/02/2023	4	7:58 AM		22/02/2023	4	7:56 AM
23/02/2023	5	8:28 AM		23/02/2023	5	8:16 AM
24/02/2023	6	8:59 AM		24/02/2023	6	8:38 AM
25/02/2023	7	9:32 AM		25/02/2023	7	9:02 AM
26/02/2023	8	10:08 AM		26/02/2023	8	9:30 AM
27/02/2023	9	10:49 AM		27/02/2023	9	10:03 AM
28/02/2023	10	11:34 AM		28/02/2023	10	10:44 AM

You can find the description of each lunar day in the chapter "A Guide to The Moon Cycle and Lunar Days"

February is a time of great beginnings, achievements, and decisive steps in all directions. Buckle up and hold on tight!

Work. This month, you will finally find yourself on an even path as you develop your ideas and projects. Business owners and managers of every level can count on successful negotiations with people with whom you recently found yourself in a deadlock. This most likely involves colleagues from other cities and abroad, who have been behaving unintelligently, if not with outright hostility for some time. Now, you are likely to finally reach an agreement with them. The best time for this is the last 20 days of the month.

During the first 10 days of the month, expect less success, and possible disagreements over work-related issues, which you will overcome sometime later. You might bring in intermediaries or allies to help you with this, though remember your opponents may do the same. Things are sure to improve in any case and knowing that is already a lot.

Another source of difficulty in February may be your relationship with a subordinate, and any manager or person responsible for major projects should take that into account. They may not be carrying out your instructions and ideas, which is sure to harm your business.

Alternatively, you may simply have to take on some of the work yourself.

Business travel planned for February will turn out very favorably.

Money. Financially speaking, February is relatively neutral. Your income is stable, and your expenses are modest and reasonable.

Much of your spending this month is likely to be related to your home, family, and children's needs.

Love and family. There are a lot of developments in your personal life, right now. Parents are still concerned about their children. A lot of your family budget may go toward them.

Your relationship with a relative, and possibly someone who was close to you in the past, may be less than ideal. However, you will make some progress, here, and gradually, the major disagreement will be resolved, and things will return to normal.

Couples will have a rough first 10 days of the month, and conflict between Mars and Venus may lead to arguments, disappointment, and taking offense. Get through this period, and the heavens will eventually calm down and look quite differently.

Single people and those who have been disappointed in the past are sure to meet someone new. You might have a torrid affair, and if you are ready for a long-term, stable relationship, nothing is stopping you, either.

Health. You are healthy in February, energetic, and leaving a great impression on everyone fate throws your way. During the first 10 days of the month, be careful when traveling or driving.

March

New York Time			London Time		
Calendar Day	Lunar Day	Lunar Day Start Time	Calendar Day	Lunar Day	Lunar Day Start Time
01/03/2023	11	12:24 PM	01/03/2023	11	11:33 AM
02/03/2023	12	1:19 PM	02/03/2023	12	12:29 PM
03/03/2023	13	2:16 PM	03/03/2023	13	1:31 PM
04/03/2023	14	3:15 PM	04/03/2023	14	2:36 PM
05/03/2023	15	4:15 PM	05/03/2023	15	3:44 PM
06/03/2023	16	5:14 PM	06/03/2023	16	4:52 PM
07/03/2023	17	6:15 PM	07/03/2023	17	6:00 PM
08/03/2023	18	7:15 PM	08/03/2023	18	7:09 PM
09/03/2023	19	8:17 PM	09/03/2023	19	8:19 PM
10/03/2023	20	9:20 PM	10/03/2023	20	9:31 PM
11/03/2023	21	10:25 PM	11/03/2023	21	10:44 PM
13/03/2023	22	12:31 AM	12/03/2023	22	11:58 PM
14/03/2023	23	1:37 AM	14/03/2023	23	1:11 AM
15/03/2023	24	2:40 AM	15/03/2023	24	2:18 AM
16/03/2023	25	3:37 AM	16/03/2023	25	3:16 AM
17/03/2023	26	4:28 AM	17/03/2023	26	4:03 AM
18/03/2023	27	5:12 AM	18/03/2023	27	4:41 AM
19/03/2023	28	5:50 AM	19/03/2023	28	5:10 AM
20/03/2023	29	6:23 AM	20/03/2023	29	5:35 AM
21/03/2023	30	6:54 AM	21/03/2023	30	5:57 AM
21/03/2023	1	1:26 PM	21/03/2023	1	5:26 PM
22/03/2023	2	7:24 AM	22/03/2023	2	6:17 AM
23/03/2023	3	7:55 AM	23/03/2023	3	6:38 AM
24/03/2023	4	8:27 AM	24/03/2023	4	7:01 AM
25/03/2023	5	9:03 AM	25/03/2023	5	7:28 AM
26/03/2023	6	9:43 AM	26/03/2023	6	9:00 AM
27/03/2023	7	10:27 AM	27/03/2023	7	9:38 AM
28/03/2023	8	11:16 AM	28/03/2023	8	10:25 AM
29/03/2023	9	12:10 PM	29/03/2023	9	11:19 AM
30/03/2023	10	1:07 PM	30/03/2023	10	12:19 PM
31/03/2023	11	2:05 PM	31/03/2023	11	1:24 PM

You can find the description of each lunar day in the chapter "A Guide to The Moon Cycle and Lunar Days"

March is an unusual month for you. There is no better time to unravel some of your life's most complicated mysteries, intrigue, or anything analytic! In short, you are playing Sherlock Holmes more than just a little!

Work. In March, you will have to figure out how to fulfill the responsibilities you have taken on and how to get your partners to follow through with what they promised you. At first glance, it seems simple – you have plenty of well-wishers, strong arguments, and the facts are on your side.

Though it's smooth sailing during the first 10 days of the month, with no setbacks or problems, during the second 10 days, things will suddenly become more difficult. Most likely, the problems will involve partners from other cities or abroad whose hostility has been palpable for some time. This time, you will once again have to respond to various demands, workplace misunderstandings, and other issues that you cannot ignore.

This time, however, things will be resolved quickly – by the last 10 days of March, expect calm waters once again.

Managers and business owners are advised to keep an eye on their subordinates. You might have to overhaul your team and get rid of those who are not willing to support you. The sooner, the better off you will be.

Money. March is not particularly exciting when it comes to your bank account. Your income is stable, and your expenses are low. If you need it, you can count on help from loved ones who are on a successful streak.

Expect the largest sums to come in on March 1-3, 6. 11, 12. 20, 21, 29, and 30.

Love and family. March is a great time for you to tackle any issues in your personal life. Single people and those who have been let down by love in the past can count on a fateful encounter. Let nature take its course, don't try to force anything, and the stars will have your back.

Couples who get along will work together to overcome issues related to relatives who are currently experiencing difficulties.

The second 10 days of the month will be the most challenging, but by the last 10 days, many issues are likely to be resolved in your favor. This may involve your in-laws and your partner playing a key role in smoothing things over.

Any trips planned for March will be a success, especially during the first or last 10 days of the month.

Health. In March, you are not exactly bounding with energy, so lead a healthy lifestyle and take care of yourself to avoid any spring infections or colds.

March is also a great time to quit bad habits, visit a beauty salon, and take some time to enjoy nature. Despite how busy you are, you will be able to find two or three days to relax.

April

New York Time			London Time		
Calendar Day	Lunar Day	Lunar Day Start Time	Calendar Day	Lunar Day	Lunar Day Start Time
01/04/2023	12	3:04 PM	01/04/2023	12	2:30 PM
02/04/2023	13	4:04 PM	02/04/2023	13	3:38 PM
03/04/2023	14	5:04 PM	03/04/2023	14	4:46 PM
04/04/2023	15	6:05 PM	04/04/2023	15	5:56 PM
05/04/2023	16	7:07 PM	05/04/2023	16	7:06 PM
06/04/2023	17	8:11 PM	06/04/2023	17	8:18 PM
07/04/2023	18	9:16 PM	07/04/2023	18	9:32 PM
08/04/2023	19	10:23 PM	08/04/2023	19	10:47 PM
09/04/2023	20	11:30 PM	10/04/2023	20	12:02 AM
11/04/2023	21	12:34 AM	11/04/2023	21	1:11 AM
12/04/2023	22	1:33 AM	12/04/2023	22	2:12 AM
13/04/2023	23	2:25 AM	13/04/2023	23	3:02 AM
14/04/2023	24	3:10 AM	14/04/2023	24	3:41 AM
15/04/2023	25	3:48 AM	15/04/2023	25	4:12 AM
16/04/2023	26	4:22 AM	16/04/2023	26	4:38 AM
17/04/2023	27	4:53 AM	17/04/2023	27	5:00 AM
18/04/2023	28	5:22 AM	18/04/2023	28	5:20 AM
19/04/2023	29	5:52 AM	19/04/2023	29	5:40 AM
20/04/2023	1	12:15 AM	20/04/2023	1	5:15 AM
20/04/2023	2	6:23 AM	20/04/2023	2	6:02 AM
21/04/2023	3	6:57 AM	21/04/2023	3	6:27 AM
22/04/2023	4	7:35 AM	22/04/2023	4	6:56 AM
23/04/2023	5	8:18 AM	23/04/2023	5	7:32 AM
24/04/2023	6	9:06 AM	24/04/2023	6	8:15 AM
25/04/2023	7	9:59 AM	25/04/2023	7	9:07 AM
26/04/2023	8	10:55 AM	26/04/2023	8	10:06 AM
27/04/2023	9	11:53 AM	27/04/2023	9	11:09 AM
28/04/2023	10	12:52 PM	28/04/2023	10	12:15 PM
29/04/2023	11	1:52 PM	29/04/2023	11	1:23 PM
30/04/2023	12	2:51 PM	30/04/2023	12	2:30 PM

You can find the description of each lunar day in the chapter "A Guide to The Moon Cycle and Lunar Days"

April is a great time for slowing down, taking a close look at things, and analyzing your work. It is also a great time for both business and personal meetings. Plan things well in order to keep up!

Work. Business owners and managers will have to work on getting their teams in order. Upper management may be inspecting things, or you can expect new associates, which will take up most of your time at work this month. Business owners and managers will have to cut ties with those weighing them down and take a long, hard look at who is conscientious and professional. You have been thinking about this for a while now, but the time has now come for you to overhaul your team and make some changes for the better.

Employees have an opportunity to improve their position, and if that recently took place, then April is the perfect time to strengthen it further. This is a great time for meetings, new acquaintances, and discussing financial issues. The latter is especially important for those who are expanding their business.

Money. Financially, April is fairly successful for you. You will have regular income, and expect the largest sums to come in on April 8, 9, 17, 18, and 25-27.

In addition to your usual earnings, you might also hold successful negotiations on credit, loans, and sponsorship. Those who are not part of the working world can count on help from a loved one, spouse, or parents.

Love and family. Don't try to swim against the tide in your family and romantic relationships, and consider your loved one's concerns – here, your relationship is reaching a new level of understanding, trust, and love.

Single people can count on an interesting encounter at work, on your team, or among new associates. In April, the stars will give you the green light for an office romance.

Couples who get along will continue events related to buying or perhaps building a new home.

Health. In April, you are feeling sluggish, so take care of yourself and try to lead a healthy lifestyle. This is a good time for massages, a trip to the spa, or anything to take care of yourself.

You might reconsider your lifestyle and drop your bad habits if you have any, and take steps to avoid falling ill. The lord helps those who help themselves!

May

New York Time			London Time		
Calendar Day	Lunar Day	Lunar Day Start Time	Calendar Day	Lunar Day	Lunar Day Start Time
01/05/2023	13	3:52 PM	01/05/2023	13	3:39 PM
02/05/2023	14	4:53 PM	02/05/2023	14	4:48 PM
03/05/2023	15	5:56 PM	03/05/2023	15	6:00 PM
04/05/2023	16	7:02 PM	04/05/2023	16	7:14 PM
05/05/2023	17	8:09 PM	05/05/2023	17	8:30 PM
06/05/2023	18	9:18 PM	06/05/2023	18	9:47 PM
07/05/2023	19	10:25 PM	07/05/2023	19	11:00 PM
08/05/2023	20	11:27 PM	09/05/2023	20	12:06 AM
10/05/2023	21	12:22 AM	10/05/2023	21	1:01 AM
11/05/2023	22	1:10 AM	11/05/2023	22	1:43 AM
12/05/2023	23	1:50 AM	12/05/2023	23	2:16 AM
13/05/2023	24	2:24 AM	13/05/2023	24	2:43 AM
14/05/2023	25	2:55 AM	14/05/2023	25	3:05 AM
15/05/2023	26	3:24 AM	15/05/2023	26	3:25 AM
16/05/2023	27	3:53 AM	16/05/2023	27	3:45 AM
17/05/2023	28	4:23 AM	17/05/2023	28	4:05 AM
18/05/2023	29	4:55 AM	18/05/2023	29	4:28 AM
19/05/2023	30	5:31 AM	19/05/2023	30	4:55 AM
19/05/2023	1	11:55 AM	19/05/2023	1	4:55 PM
20/05/2023	2	6:11 AM	20/05/2023	2	5:27 AM
21/05/2023	3	6:57 AM	21/05/2023	3	6:08 AM
22/05/2023	4	7:48 AM	22/05/2023	4	6:56 AM
23/05/2023	5	8:44 AM	23/05/2023	5	7:53 AM
24/05/2023	6	9:42 AM	24/05/2023	6	8:55 AM
25/05/2023	7	10:41 AM	25/05/2023	7	10:01 AM
26/05/2023	8	11:40 AM	26/05/2023	8	11:07 AM
27/05/2023	9	12:39 PM	27/05/2023	9	12:14 PM
28/05/2023	10	1:38 PM	28/05/2023	10	1:22 PM
29/05/2023	11	2:38 PM	29/05/2023	11	2:30 PM
30/05/2023	12	3:39 PM	30/05/2023	12	3:40 PM
31/05/2023	13	4:43 PM	31/05/2023	13	4:52 PM

You can find the description of each lunar day in the chapter "A Guide to The Moon Cycle and Lunar Days"

May is a time of anxiety and transitions for you. You may be a subtle and romantic Libra, but right now you are shouldering something unusual for you – household and domestic tasks.

Work. During the first 20 days of May, you may run into some hurdles at work. Don't expect a breakthrough at work, but you might be planning things and giving your work a thorough review.

Business owners and managers should focus on finances and keep a scrupulous record of everything.

You might make large expenditures on expanding your business, maybe acquiring land or facilities for that purpose. You can expect a lot of work to deal with all year long. The stars welcome any negotiations with partners, banks, and other financial institutions.

Your relationship with colleagues in other cities or abroad is noticeably improved, and you might be holding discussions that seem lengthy, but will bring positive results.

Employees be busy with family matters, which are also going through a time of transitions.

The last 10 days of May are the best time for anything work-related, when things will move forward smoothly and efficiently.

Money. Financially, you are doing great in May. You might not be making your own money, but you can count on funds from business partners, favorable credit, and help along the way.

You might also get support from your spouse or a loved one.

Love and family. There are major changes in your family life, right now. Many Libras are totally or partially changing up their residence. For example, you might be moving to a new home, buying an apartment, summer home, or working on major repairs.

Some Libras are already making strides in this direction this month, while others will be busy with this project all year long.

Many families are experiencing difficulties related to children. Adult children may be growing emotionally distant, while you need to watch small ones like a hawk!

After a lot of ups and downs, unmarried couples might decide to live together and be discussing both romantic and financial issues.

Any trips planned for the first 20 days of May will go well, as long as you select a destination you have been to many times before.

Health. In May, you are not as energetic as you have been, so lead a healthy lifestyle and remember to get enough sleep!

June

New York Time			London Time		
Calendar Day	Lunar Day	Lunar Day Start Time	Calendar Day	Lunar Day	Lunar Day Start Time
01/06/2023	14	5:50 PM	01/06/2023	14	6:07 PM
02/06/2023	15	6:59 PM	02/06/2023	15	7:24 PM
03/06/2023	16	8:08 PM	03/06/2023	16	8:41 PM
04/06/2023	17	9:14 PM	04/06/2023	17	9:52 PM
05/06/2023	18	10:14 PM	05/06/2023	18	10:53 PM
06/06/2023	19	11:06 PM	06/06/2023	19	11:41 PM
07/06/2023	20	11:50 PM	08/06/2023	20	12:19 AM
09/06/2023	21	12:27 AM	09/06/2023	21	12:48 AM
10/06/2023	22	12:59 AM	10/06/2023	22	1:11 AM
11/06/2023	23	1:29 AM	11/06/2023	23	1:32 AM
12/06/2023	24	1:57 AM	12/06/2023	24	1:52 AM
13/06/2023	25	2:26 AM	13/06/2023	25	2:11 AM
14/06/2023	26	2:56 AM	14/06/2023	26	2:33 AM
15/06/2023	27	3:30 AM	15/06/2023	27	2:57 AM
16/06/2023	28	4:08 AM	16/06/2023	28	3:27 AM
17/06/2023	29	4:51 AM	17/06/2023	29	4:04 AM
18/06/2023	1	12:39 AM	18/06/2023	30	4:49 AM
18/06/2023	2	5:40 AM	18/06/2023	1	5:39 AM
19/06/2023	3	6:34 AM	19/06/2023	2	5:42 AM
20/06/2023	4	7:31 AM	20/06/2023	3	6:43 AM
21/06/2023	5	8:30 AM	21/06/2023	4	7:47 AM
22/06/2023	6	9:29 AM	22/06/2023	5	8:54 AM
23/06/2023	7	10:28 AM	23/06/2023	6	10:01 AM
24/06/2023	8	11:27 AM	24/06/2023	7	11:07 AM
25/06/2023	9	12:25 PM	25/06/2023	8	12:14 PM
26/06/2023	10	1:25 PM	26/06/2023	9	1:22 PM
27/06/2023	11	2:27 PM	27/06/2023	10	2:32 PM
28/06/2023	12	3:31 PM	28/06/2023	11	3:44 PM
29/06/2023	13	4:37 PM	29/06/2023	12	4:59 PM
30/06/2023	14	5:46 PM	30/06/2023	13	6:15 PM

You can find the description of each lunar day in the chapter "A Guide to The Moon Cycle and Lunar Days"

You are embarking on a fast-moving, dynamic, and extremely practical month. You want a lot, and nothing is stopping you from getting it! The heavens are on your side!

Work. In June, you are busy with every day, administrative, and financial tasks. Business owners and managers at every level will be holding important negotiations with partners and the results will be positive.

You might be actively cooperating with colleagues from other cities or abroad. You may even go on a successful trip!

Despite the generally positive tone this month, there is no way to avoid trouble entirely. This time, the fly in the ointment might be a difficult relationship with a colleague or your subordinates. They may throw a wrench in your plans, which will slow down everything. This is a longstanding problem, and perhaps you will decide it is time to change things up. This is what severe Saturn, which has been in the sector of your sky related to work, recommends.

Money. Financially, June is a favorable time for you, not so much because of your own resources, but because you will be able to count on material support from business partners, credit, or even income from unofficial sources.

Those who are not part of the working world might count on support from a loved one who is experiencing a positive streak at work.

Some Libras will receive an inheritance.

Expect some expenses related to your children's needs, as well as those of people in your circle. They may be so-called "friends" or people who are highly placed in society. The stars have some advice, here: do not promise too much, because their appetites may grow.

Love and family. Many Libras may be busy with everyday household issues. Major home repairs, selling real estate, buying other property, and other stressful tasks are on the agenda. That may happen in another city or abroad.

Your relationship with your children has been rocky in the past, and most likely, they are already adults, if that is the case. You are well-aware of the reason for this tension, so there is nothing new, here. You may temporarily fall out with a family member, as well.

Couples' relationships are also difficult, this month, and in the worst cases, they may separate. If there is any love still alive, it is worth trying to stick together, but otherwise, whatever happens, happens.

Health. This month, you are not as healthy as you could be, and the time has come to begin taking your well-being seriously.

Those who are young and strong should lead a healthy lifestyle, but the elderly and those who are weakened might take some preventive measures against chronic conditions, which will be prone to resurfacing.

July

New York Time			London Time		
Calendar Day	Lunar Day	Lunar Day Start Time	Calendar Day	Lunar Day	Lunar Day Start Time
01/07/2023	15	6:54 PM	01/07/2023	14	7:30 PM
02/07/2023	16	7:58 PM	02/07/2023	15	8:37 PM
03/07/2023	17	8:55 PM	03/07/2023	16	9:33 PM
04/07/2023	18	9:44 PM	04/07/2023	17	10:16 PM
05/07/2023	19	10:25 PM	05/07/2023	18	10:49 PM
06/07/2023	20	11:00 PM	06/07/2023	19	11:15 PM
07/07/2023	21	11:31 PM	07/07/2023	20	11:38 PM
09/07/2023	22	12:01 AM	08/07/2023	21	11:58 PM
10/07/2023	23	12:29 AM	10/07/2023	22	12:18 AM
11/07/2023	24	12:59 AM	11/07/2023	23	12:39 AM
12/07/2023	25	1:32 AM	12/07/2023	24	1:02 AM
13/07/2023	26	2:08 AM	13/07/2023	25	1:30 AM
14/07/2023	27	2:49 AM	14/07/2023	26	2:04 AM
15/07/2023	28	3:36 AM	15/07/2023	27	2:46 AM
16/07/2023	29	4:28 AM	16/07/2023	28	3:36 AM
17/07/2023	30	5:24 AM	17/07/2023	29	4:34 AM
17/07/2023	1	2:33 PM	17/07/2023	1	7:33 PM
18/07/2023	2	6:22 AM	18/07/2023	2	5:37 AM
19/07/2023	3	7:21 AM	19/07/2023	3	6:43 AM
20/07/2023	4	8:20 AM	20/07/2023	4	7:50 AM
21/07/2023	5	9:19 AM	21/07/2023	5	8:56 AM
22/07/2023	6	10:17 AM	22/07/2023	6	10:03 AM
23/07/2023	7	11:15 AM	23/07/2023	7	11:09 AM
24/07/2023	8	12:15 PM	24/07/2023	8	12:17 PM
25/07/2023	9	1:16 PM	25/07/2023	9	1:27 PM
26/07/2023	10	2:20 PM	26/07/2023	10	2:39 PM
27/07/2023	11	3:26 PM	27/07/2023	11	3:53 PM
28/07/2023	12	4:33 PM	28/07/2023	12	5:07 PM
29/07/2023	13	5:39 PM	29/07/2023	13	6:16 PM
30/07/2023	14	6:39 PM	30/07/2023	14	7:17 PM
31/07/2023	15	7:32 PM	31/07/2023	15	8:07 PM

You can find the description of each lunar day in the chapter "A Guide to The Moon Cycle and Lunar Days"

July has its ups and downs for you. You will make achievements, but nothing comes without some baggage. But remember – you never know what you are capable of until you try.

Work. In July, you will have to work hard to defend your place in the sun.

Many Libras will be dealing with unresolved tasks that began in 2022. That includes a relationship with a like-minded person, and various financial obligations. In some cases, it may be problems between the two of you, and it could involve friends or possibly people highly placed in society with material claims, and you will have to settle up. Things will be at their sharpest during the first 10 days of the month, however thanks to your hard work and efforts, you will manage to push through.

During the last 10 days of the month, you will face problems of a different sort. Business owners and managers at every level will face opposition from their subordinates, while employees may have to grapple with an ill-intentioned colleague.

Many Libras will have to contend with secret enemies and those who are in open conflict with you. If this is the case, the last 10 days of the month will be particularly telling. This situation may continue into the future, so keep your fingers on the pulse of what is happening and be sure to keep an eye on yourself.

Money. Despite the trouble at work, you will not find yourself in the red. Your income compensates for your expenses, and close to the end of July, your bank account will be neutral.

Love and family. July is heavily focused on your professional life, and you may not have much time left over for personal matters. In many families, you will be talking about major household changes, and that may keep you busy with your spouse or loved one.

Most likely, you are building a home, apartment, summer home, or buying new real estate. In some cases, this may continue into next year or take place in another country.

Relationships in dysfunctional families are far from ideal. You may see conflict related to money or disagreements over how to raise your children. It is likely that some secrets – either yours or your partner's – will come to light, which will not help smooth things over with your family. If that is your case, be careful and do not behave suspiciously or give anyone any reason to gossip.

Unmarried couples may experience a similar situation, but here, this only concerns partners who have faced many problems in the past.

Health. In July, you are healthy, energetic, and this means you are able to favorably resolve any problems that life throws at you, whether at work or at home.

August

New York Time			London Time		
Calendar Day	Lunar Day	Lunar Day Start Time	Calendar Day	Lunar Day	Lunar Day Start Time
01/08/2023	16	8:17 PM	01/08/2023	16	8:45 PM
02/08/2023	17	8:56 PM	02/08/2023	17	9:15 PM
03/08/2023	18	9:30 PM	03/08/2023	18	9:40 PM
04/08/2023	19	10:01 PM	04/08/2023	19	10:02 PM
05/08/2023	20	10:31 PM	05/08/2023	20	10:22 PM
06/08/2023	21	11:01 PM	06/08/2023	21	10:44 PM
07/08/2023	22	11:33 PM	07/08/2023	22	11:07 PM
09/08/2023	23	12:09 AM	08/08/2023	23	11:33 PM
10/08/2023	24	12:49 AM	10/08/2023	24	12:05 AM
11/08/2023	25	1:34 AM	11/08/2023	25	12:44 AM
12/08/2023	26	2:24 AM	12/08/2023	26	1:32 AM
13/08/2023	27	3:18 AM	13/08/2023	27	2:27 AM
14/08/2023	28	4:16 AM	14/08/2023	28	3:29 AM
15/08/2023	29	5:14 AM	15/08/2023	29	4:34 AM
16/08/2023	1	5:38 AM	15/08/2023	30	5:41 AM
16/08/2023	2	6:13 AM	16/08/2023	1	10:38 AM
17/08/2023	3	7:12 AM	17/08/2023	2	6:47 AM
18/08/2023	4	8:10 AM	18/08/2023	3	7:54 AM
19/08/2023	5	9:09 AM	19/08/2023	4	9:00 AM
20/08/2023	6	10:08 AM	20/08/2023	5	10:07 AM
21/08/2023	7	11:08 AM	21/08/2023	6	11:16 AM
22/08/2023	8	12:10 PM	22/08/2023	7	12:25 PM
23/08/2023	9	1:13 PM	23/08/2023	8	1:37 PM
24/08/2023	10	2:18 PM	24/08/2023	9	2:49 PM
25/08/2023	11	3:22 PM	25/08/2023	10	3:59 PM
26/08/2023	12	4:23 PM	26/08/2023	11	5:02 PM
27/08/2023	13	5:18 PM	27/08/2023	12	5:56 PM
28/08/2023	14	6:06 PM	28/08/2023	13	6:38 PM
29/08/2023	15	6:48 PM	29/08/2023	14	7:12 PM
30/08/2023	16	7:24 PM	30/08/2023	15	7:39 PM
31/08/2023	17	7:57 PM	31/08/2023	16	8:03 PM

You can find the description of each lunar day in the chapter "A Guide to The Moon Cycle and Lunar Days"

The road to success is not always strewn with rose petals. But it is still there, and your job is to find it in the confusing labyrinth of life.

Work. You will spend much of August relaxing, somewhere with a warm, sunny beach. But if you absolutely cannot step away from work, the stars still recommend that you get your affairs in order, especially financial matters.

All month long, you may be bleeding money for various reasons. If you have debts, obligations to like-minded people, highly placed individuals, or friends, this is the time to settle them.

Another concern this month will be your relationship with your team at work, and you might expect conflicts with certain associates. This is nothing new to you, and certainly not the first time that these people have displayed such shortcomings. You should have made a change long ago, but nothing is stopping you from doing it right now.

Employees might see trouble brewing on their team, and the best thing you can do is show restraint and avoid any intrigue.

This month, beware of rumors, gossip, and unpleasant secrets, both yours and those around you. This may not be resolved until next month.

Money. August will leave your bank account in ruins. Your money will be burning a hole in your pocket, and this time, the culprit may be work, debts, or possibly your personal life, including recreation or your family's and children's needs.

You can be sure to count on support from a loved one who is experiencing a lucky streak at work.

Young people can count on their parents or older family members.

Love and family. Many Libras will be focused on relaxation during these dog days of summer. You can expect fun outings with friends, shopping, and the joy of forgetting about work and instead spending time with your loved ones and family – all you need in August.

Those planning any major construction or repairs might spend the lion's share of the family budget on these endeavors.

For lovers, the sky above you may be grey and cloudy in August. Your ruler, Venus, will be in retrograde all month long, so expect doubts and hesitations in your relationship, as well. If things remain cool, that may become dangerous. Keep that in mind, and if you want to save your relationship, be pure as a dove and wise as an owl. Avoid gossip and intrigue.

Health. In August, be especially careful if you are elderly or suffer from chronic conditions. The stars recommend you be attentive to your body, especially during the last 10 days of the month.

September

New York Time			London Time		
Calendar Day	Lunar Day	Lunar Day Start Time	Calendar Day	Lunar Day	Lunar Day Start Time
01/09/2023	18	8:28 PM	01/09/2023	17	8:24 PM
02/09/2023	19	8:59 PM	02/09/2023	18	8:46 PM
03/09/2023	20	9:32 PM	03/09/2023	19	9:09 PM
04/09/2023	21	10:07 PM	04/09/2023	20	9:34 PM
05/09/2023	22	10:46 PM	05/09/2023	21	10:05 PM
06/09/2023	23	11:30 PM	06/09/2023	22	10:43 PM
08/09/2023	24	12:19 AM	07/09/2023	23	11:28 PM
09/09/2023	25	1:13 AM	09/09/2023	24	12:21 AM
10/09/2023	26	2:09 AM	10/09/2023	25	1:21 AM
11/09/2023	27	3:08 AM	11/09/2023	26	2:25 AM
12/09/2023	28	4:07 AM	12/09/2023	27	3:31 AM
13/09/2023	29	5:05 AM	13/09/2023	28	4:38 AM
14/09/2023	30	6:04 AM	14/09/2023	29	5:45 AM
14/09/2023	1	9:40 PM	15/09/2023	1	2:40 AM
15/09/2023	2	7:03 AM	15/09/2023	2	6:52 AM
16/09/2023	3	8:02 AM	16/09/2023	3	7:59 AM
17/09/2023	4	9:02 AM	17/09/2023	4	9:07 AM
18/09/2023	5	10:03 AM	18/09/2023	5	10:16 AM
19/09/2023	6	11:06 AM	19/09/2023	6	11:27 AM
20/09/2023	7	12:10 PM	20/09/2023	7	12:39 PM
21/09/2023	8	1:13 PM	21/09/2023	8	1:48 PM
22/09/2023	9	2:13 PM	22/09/2023	9	2:52 PM
23/09/2023	10	3:09 PM	23/09/2023	10	3:48 PM
24/09/2023	11	3:58 PM	24/09/2023	11	4:33 PM
25/09/2023	12	4:41 PM	25/09/2023	12	5:09 PM
26/09/2023	13	5:18 PM	26/09/2023	13	5:38 PM
27/09/2023	14	5:52 PM	27/09/2023	14	6:03 PM
28/09/2023	15	6:24 PM	28/09/2023	15	6:25 PM
29/09/2023	16	6:55 PM	29/09/2023	16	6:46 PM
30/09/2023	17	7:27 PM	30/09/2023	17	7:08 PM

You can find the description of each lunar day in the chapter "A Guide to The Moon Cycle and Lunar Days"

After a busy, hectic summer, the pendulum has swung to the other side. You might become slow and judicious, but that is the right path, right now – you will have far less errors to deal with.

Work. During the first two weeks of September, you can expect to run into some hiccups. You might have trouble at work, perhaps gossip involving competitors, and secret foes at play.

Managers and business owners are advised to keep an eye on their subordinates, as not everything is as it should be here. The planets predict that during the first half of the month, some of the people who should support you will display their shortcomings, which might make things significantly more difficult for you at work.

Alternatively, this might go beyond the matter of one forgetting his or her obligations, and into outright treachery. Look at all your options and take any measures you can.

Any events related to expanding your business, including major repairs or acquiring land or other real estate will turn out well. If you are purchasing something, it is best to wait until after September 15.

A difficult relationship with a friend or someone highly placed in society will be smoothed over. If the issue involves an argument over finances, you are sure to reach a compromise.

Money. When it comes to money, September is a positive month for you. You may have income from unofficial sources, including support from a loved one, parents, or instead receive credit or profit from a beneficial real estate transaction or an inheritance.

Love and family. In many cases, your personal life is more important than work right now. Your home is your castle, and most Libras are well aware of that. You might be busy with major repairs, buying a home, apartment, or summer home. In some cases, this began recently and is now reaching its logical conclusion.

Your relationship with your partner is looking wobbly, but there is a light at the end of the tunnel. Though things will be difficult and confusing as the month begins, after September 15, things will be much clearer. You might find a way to reconcile, or perhaps, in the most extreme cases, pressure from the stars will drive you to decide to end your relationship.

Health. The last month before your birthday is usually a time when one feels sluggish, and against that backdrop, you are likely to see old illnesses flare up again. Remember that and take care of yourself.

October

New York Time			London Time		
Calendar Day	Lunar Day	Lunar Day Start Time	Calendar Day	Lunar Day	Lunar Day Start Time
01/10/2023	18	8:02 PM	01/10/2023	18	7:33 PM
02/10/2023	19	8:40 PM	02/10/2023	19	8:02 PM
03/10/2023	20	9:23 PM	03/10/2023	20	8:38 PM
04/10/2023	21	10:11 PM	04/10/2023	21	9:21 PM
05/10/2023	22	11:04 PM	05/10/2023	22	10:12 PM
07/10/2023	23	12:01 AM	06/10/2023	23	11:11 PM
08/10/2023	24	12:59 AM	08/10/2023	24	12:14 AM
09/10/2023	25	1:58 AM	09/10/2023	25	1:20 AM
10/10/2023	26	2:57 AM	10/10/2023	26	2:27 AM
11/10/2023	27	3:56 AM	11/10/2023	27	3:34 AM
12/10/2023	28	4:54 AM	12/10/2023	28	4:40 AM
13/10/2023	29	5:54 AM	13/10/2023	29	5:48 AM
14/10/2023	30	6:54 AM	14/10/2023	30	6:56 AM
14/10/2023	1	1:55 PM	14/10/2023	1	6:55 PM
15/10/2023	2	7:55 AM	15/10/2023	2	8:06 AM
16/10/2023	3	8:59 AM	16/10/2023	3	9:17 AM
17/10/2023	4	10:03 AM	17/10/2023	4	10:29 AM
18/10/2023	5	11:07 AM	18/10/2023	5	11:40 AM
19/10/2023	6	12:08 PM	19/10/2023	6	12:46 PM
20/10/2023	7	1:05 PM	20/10/2023	7	1:44 PM
21/10/2023	8	1:55 PM	21/10/2023	8	2:32 PM
22/10/2023	9	2:38 PM	22/10/2023	9	3:09 PM
23/10/2023	10	3:16 PM	23/10/2023	10	3:40 PM
24/10/2023	11	3:50 PM	24/10/2023	11	4:05 PM
25/10/2023	12	4:21 PM	25/10/2023	12	4:27 PM
26/10/2023	13	4:51 PM	26/10/2023	13	4:48 PM
27/10/2023	14	5:22 PM	27/10/2023	14	5:09 PM
28/10/2023	15	5:55 PM	28/10/2023	15	5:32 PM
29/10/2023	16	6:32 PM	29/10/2023	16	4:59 PM
30/10/2023	17	7:13 PM	30/10/2023	17	5:31 PM
31/10/2023	18	8:00 PM	31/10/2023	18	6:11 PM

You can find the description of each lunar day in the chapter "A Guide to The Moon Cycle and Lunar Days"

In October, you will prove yourself to be a tough boss and a total materialist. There is nothing you can do about that – it is the only way for you to solve a lot of problems. Since you are on the right path, the stars are sure to lend a hand!

Work. In October, many Libras will have a nice opportunity to resolve some of the difficulties that cropped up in September. Business owners are slowly but surely continuing to expand their business, and this month, you will be able to make several steps in that direction. You are still carrying out various transactions involving real estate, land, or other large property.

Not everything will go the way you had planned and hoped this month. Business owners and managers should be attentive with their subordinates, and employees should do the same with their colleagues. Right now, things are looking relatively easy, but disagreements are still likely. A mistake by someone who should be supporting you may end up costing you dearly.

This month, you would be wise to watch your back, as information you'd rather keep in the dark may surface.

Money. Financially, October is full of ups and downs. You will not end up bankrupt, but your expenses are high. The last 10 days of the month are especially acute here, when you can expect to be bleeding money. That may be related to work and expanding your business, or possibly with resolving issues at home and with your family.

Love and family. Things are not all rosy in your personal life. Couples who get along will be busy improving their home, and things will not go as planned. You may not agree on how you want your future home to look or how much to spend, and you may end up arguing, which will not end until you are done with the project.

You are likely to bicker over money, especially after October 20. Be careful and avoid pressuring your loved one. Mars is in your sign for almost the entire month, and it brings aggression and sudden moves. That might be a good quality at work, but it is less than ideal in your personal life.

All Libras should keep that in mind, whether they are married or not. Your sign's greatest skill is patience and an ability to be both diplomatic and delicate. Don't lose sight of that, and things will go much better for you.

Health. You are healthy, energetic, and busy this month, and no illness can keep you down.

November

New York Time			London Time		
Calendar Day	Lunar Day	Lunar Day Start Time	Calendar Day	Lunar Day	Lunar Day Start Time
01/11/2023	19	8:52 PM	01/11/2023	19	7:00 PM
02/11/2023	20	9:49 PM	02/11/2023	20	7:57 PM
03/11/2023	21	10:47 PM	03/11/2023	21	9:00 PM
04/11/2023	22	11:47 PM	04/11/2023	22	10:06 PM
05/11/2023	23	11:46 PM	05/11/2023	23	11:13 PM
07/11/2023	24	12:45 AM	07/11/2023	24	12:20 AM
08/11/2023	25	1:43 AM	08/11/2023	25	1:26 AM
09/11/2023	26	2:42 AM	09/11/2023	26	2:33 AM
10/11/2023	27	3:42 AM	10/11/2023	27	3:41 AM
11/11/2023	28	4:43 AM	11/11/2023	28	4:50 AM
12/11/2023	29	5:46 AM	12/11/2023	29	6:02 AM
13/11/2023	1	4:27 AM	13/11/2023	30	7:15 AM
13/11/2023	2	6:51 AM	13/11/2023	1	9:27 AM
14/11/2023	3	7:57 AM	14/11/2023	2	8:28 AM
15/11/2023	4	9:01 AM	15/11/2023	3	9:38 AM
16/11/2023	5	10:00 AM	16/11/2023	4	10:40 AM
17/11/2023	6	10:53 AM	17/11/2023	5	11:31 AM
18/11/2023	7	11:39 AM	18/11/2023	6	12:12 PM
19/11/2023	8	12:18 PM	19/11/2023	7	12:44 PM
20/11/2023	9	12:52 PM	20/11/2023	8	1:10 PM
21/11/2023	10	1:23 PM	21/11/2023	9	1:32 PM
22/11/2023	11	1:52 PM	22/11/2023	10	1:52 PM
23/11/2023	12	2:22 PM	23/11/2023	11	2:12 PM
24/11/2023	13	2:53 PM	24/11/2023	12	2:34 PM
25/11/2023	14	3:27 PM	25/11/2023	13	2:58 PM
26/11/2023	15	4:05 PM	26/11/2023	14	3:27 PM
27/11/2023	16	4:49 PM	27/11/2023	15	4:03 PM
28/11/2023	17	5:39 PM	28/11/2023	16	4:48 PM
29/11/2023	18	6:35 PM	29/11/2023	17	5:42 PM
30/11/2023	19	7:33 PM	30/11/2023	18	6:43 PM

You can find the description of each lunar day in the chapter "A Guide to The Moon Cycle and Lunar Days"

All month long, you will need to stand up for your views and defend your values. They may be either moral or material in nature.

Work. November is a busy, active, and very productive month for you at work. Those who are busy expanding their business might make a lot of headway in this direction this month.

You are likely to face large expenses related to the scale of this kind of event, and that may lead to disagreements with your partners. The most challenging conversations about this will take place during the second 10 days of the month, if they happen at all. A compromise is possible, but you will have to be the one making an effort in this direction.

Your relationship with colleagues in other cities or abroad is moving along with varying success, and the biggest problems will rear their heads after November 20, when clashing views on your cooperation together might spill over into a serious conflict.

All month long, managers would do well to keep an eye on their subordinates, and employees should do the same with their colleagues. You have needed to monitor this part of your job for some time now, and you need to take steps now, before it is too late.

Money. Your financial outlook is unstable this month. You will be spending constantly, perhaps due to your business development, or alternatively, your personal life. In any case, be careful during the second ten days of the month, when you may experience financial loss in addition to all of your spending.

Love and family. Your personal life is no less busy than work in November. You are still seeing the continuation of events related to improving your home, and this time, they will cost a pretty penny. In some cases, spouses may have a serious disagreement, with the worst likely to take place between November 10 and 20. You are making mountains out of molehills, however – the family budget is able to comfortably cover any of these growing expenses.

Health. This month, you are feeling sluggish, and this will be most noticeable during the New Moon from November 12 to 14. Be attentive during the second 10 days of the month, as the likelihood of injury and accident is rather high.

December

New York Time			London Time		
Calendar Day	Lunar Day	Lunar Day Start Time	Calendar Day	Lunar Day	Lunar Day Start Time
01/12/2023	20	8:33 PM	01/12/2023	19	7:49 PM
02/12/2023	21	9:34 PM	02/12/2023	20	8:57 PM
03/12/2023	22	10:33 PM	03/12/2023	21	10:04 PM
04/12/2023	23	11:31 PM	04/12/2023	22	11:11 PM
06/12/2023	24	12:29 AM	06/12/2023	23	12:17 AM
07/12/2023	25	1:28 AM	07/12/2023	24	1:24 AM
08/12/2023	26	2:28 AM	08/12/2023	25	2:32 AM
09/12/2023	27	3:30 AM	09/12/2023	26	3:42 AM
10/12/2023	28	4:34 AM	10/12/2023	27	4:54 AM
11/12/2023	29	5:40 AM	11/12/2023	28	6:08 AM
12/12/2023	30	6:46 AM	12/12/2023	29	7:21 AM
12/12/2023	1	6:32 PM	12/12/2023	1	11:32 PM
13/12/2023	2	7:49 AM	13/12/2023	2	8:28 AM
14/12/2023	3	8:46 AM	14/12/2023	3	9:25 AM
15/12/2023	4	9:36 AM	15/12/2023	4	10:11 AM
16/12/2023	5	10:18 AM	16/12/2023	5	10:47 AM
17/12/2023	6	10:55 AM	17/12/2023	6	11:15 AM
18/12/2023	7	11:27 AM	18/12/2023	7	11:38 AM
19/12/2023	8	11:56 AM	19/12/2023	8	11:59 AM
20/12/2023	9	12:25 PM	20/12/2023	9	12:19 PM
21/12/2023	10	12:55 PM	21/12/2023	10	12:39 PM
22/12/2023	11	1:27 PM	22/12/2023	11	1:02 PM
23/12/2023	12	2:02 PM	23/12/2023	12	1:28 PM
24/12/2023	13	2:43 PM	24/12/2023	13	2:00 PM
25/12/2023	14	3:30 PM	25/12/2023	14	2:41 PM
26/12/2023	15	4:23 PM	26/12/2023	15	3:30 PM
27/12/2023	16	5:20 PM	27/12/2023	16	4:28 PM
28/12/2023	17	6:20 PM	28/12/2023	17	5:33 PM
29/12/2023	18	7:21 PM	29/12/2023	18	6:40 PM
30/12/2023	19	8:21 PM	30/12/2023	19	7:48 PM
31/12/2023	20	9:20 PM	31/12/2023	20	8:56 PM

You can find the description of each lunar day in the chapter "A Guide to The Moon Cycle and Lunar Days"

Some work that you recently completed will bear its fruit this month. You will get what you want, if not this year, in 2024. Your prize awaits!

Work. Your main task this month will be improving your relationship with colleagues in other cities or abroad. Here, you will once again deal with problems that require your attention and efforts. This will be the underlying issue of a conflict that breaks out in December. But remember, it's not as bad as it looks, so you will manage to overcome this before the month ends, and you can tie up any loose ends later.

Those who are busy expanding their business are advised to be careful with any documents, especially if they have anything to do with money.

From December 13 to January 2, Mercury, the planet that rules connections and contacts, will be in retrograde, so you will have to come back to the same issues time and again, and reconsider and implement corrections to your current projects.

Managers and business owners are still advised to keep a close eye on their subordinates, and consider changing up your team, if you can. This is a thorny issue that has been bothering you for some time, so take the stars' advice more seriously. It is not worth trying to build something with people when you just don't trust each other.

Employees might be thinking about a new job and taking steps in that direction. However, it is not quite time for that right now, so just look at your options and don't be afraid to walk away from what you have now.

Money. Financially, December is full of ups and downs. On one hand, you will not end up bankrupt, on the other, you are spending a lot. The main reason for this is expanding your business or working on your home. Here, every heart knows its own bitterness.

Love and family. Your personal life is not less active than work, this month. You are still busy setting up or improving your home, and this means your expenses are continuing along with these difficult obstacles.

However, some of those issues may already be resolved, which means lower expenses for you. A conflict in your family is not particularly likely, but there may be periodic outbursts.

Those planning on purchasing real estate in another country will deal with serious issues this month. They include foreign laws and organizational tasks.

Your relationship with relatives is still rocky, and in many cases, this may involve your in-laws. You may be able to solve this, or perhaps you will once again be taking your gloves off for a fight.

Health. In December, you are feeling energetic and have no reason to fear falling ill. However, all month long, the stars advise you to be more careful when traveling and driving.

Libra Description

Sign. Masculine, air, cardinal.

Ruler. Venus.

Exaltation. Saturn, Uranus.

Temperament. Sanguine.

Positive traits. Diplomatic, intuitive, loves harmony, idealist, romantic, friendly, tender, fair, noble, light, refined, drawn to beauty, needs a partner.

Negative traits. Lacks self-confidence, volatile, unbalanced, sensitive, weak-willed, detached from reality.

Weaknesses in the body. Groin, uterus, bladder, kidneys, thighs, skin, veins.

Metal. Copper.

Minerals. For a talisman- orange topaz. Generally- hyacinth, orange corundum, diamond, rock crystal, coral.

Numbers. 6, 8, 12.

Day. Friday.

Color. Red-orange and green blue.

Libra energy

Libra is ruled by two planets – Venus (the planet of love, beauty, and prosperity) and Chiron (the symbol of balance and justice). Venus is known to astrologists as "small happiness" (Jupiter is known as "big happiness"). Venus's energy brings Libras good luck, but behind the scenes, Libras need to work hard. They achieve much thanks to their talents, charms, persuasiveness, and ability to smooth over any contradictions. Chiron gives them the key to all kinds of information. Libras can combine that which seems incompatible – they manage to work two jobs, bring enemies and friends together, and maintain a balance, all the while.

The element of air starts off active, before getting carried away. It brings Libra the ability to keep a cool head, remain calm, and seek compromises while getting along with others and avoiding causing a conflict.

Astrological portrait of Libra

Libras are connoisseurs of beauty, aesthetics, and they strive to find the golden mean in everything. Their contradictory natures make it difficult to achieve complete harmony. Libras love people but hate crowds. They are kind and sociable while also experiencing long bouts of depression. They can be intelligent but naïve. Restless and mobile, but never in a hurry. They do not tolerate rudeness but are capable of saying a harsh word in their hearts. It is worth noting that this kind of behavior is just a mask to hide their insecurities. In fact, Libras are good-natured, and any rudeness is contrived rather than their nature. Libra's character is constantly changing, balancing, and rushing from one extreme to the next. From the outside, they may seem to be connected to two totally different people, and they might even appear confused with their own beliefs.

Libras seek stability, comfort, companionship, and partnership. However, they are selective in their contacts, and always keep a relationship with the powers that be. People lacking in intelligence are not attractive to a Libra.

Libras can only flourish in an environment of benevolence and approval.

Disharmonious and stressful situations drive them to depression and illness. They try to avoid conflicts and remove any negative energy from themselves. During a heated debate, they will usually side with the winner. At his highest level, Libra is a talented diplomat. Many politicians who manage to straddle two positions at once or provoke two sides in order to benefit from their hostility are also Libras. Despite their conflict avoidance, Libras love to argue for any reason. They take to debates like a fish to water, and always have the last word.

Libras often face contradictory situations. They have a hard time making a choice life puts in front of them. Libra's indecisiveness can be felt everywhere. They hesitate for a long time before making the right decision, and prefer to wait until things have resolved themselves, if they can.

Libras' coldness and detachment can cause them great harm. A lack of positive emotions and rigidity can have a negative impact on their Fate. A Libra's cosmic task is to learn to be sensitive and strike a balance.

Disharmony and imbalance have a very negative impact on Libra. They need to learn the essence of the phenomena around them and understand the cause-and-effect relationship. Chaos takes this ability away from Libra, and they cannot find harmony.

Most Libras have a perfectly developed ability to concentrate in order to make the right choices. They tend to be very wise people, especially in terms of life experience.

Libra's most serious shortcoming is a tendency toward stereotypical thinking and a rigid commitment to principles.

How to recognize Libra from appearances

The only thing that would distinguish a Libra from the other signs by appearance is a charming smile – it is soft, gentle, and mysterious. Libra's figure is balanced, and as a rule he does not tend to put on weight. His appearance is elusive. Wherever he goes, he changes to fit his environment, like a chameleon. Libra is careful with his appearance and is always dressed tastefully. Female Libras need to remember not to get carried away with makeup.

Charting Libra's Fate

Libra is constantly shifting from one direction to another, and so periods of happiness and prosperity are replaced with moments of sadness or disappointment. Libras tend to find prosperity in the second half of their lives. By and large, Fortune is on Libra's side, but Libra's task is to realize this and accept what he has been given.

A Guide to The Moon Cycle and Lunar Days

Since Ancient times, people have noticed that the moon has a strong influence on nature. Our Earth and everything living on it is a single living being, which is why the phases of the moon have such an effect on our health and mental state, and therefore, our lives. Remember Shakespeare and his description of Othello's jealousy in his famous tragedy:

"It is the very error of the moon, She comes more nearer Earth than she was wont And makes men mad."

If our inner rhythm is in harmony with that of the cosmos, we are able to achieve much more. People were aware of this a thousand years ago. The lunar calendar is ancient. We can find it among the ancient Sumerians (4000-3000 BC), the inhabitants of Mesopotamia, Native Americans, Hindus, and ancient Slavs. There is evidence that the Siberian Yakuts had a lunar calendar, as did the Malaysians.

Primitive tribes saw the moon as a source of fertility. Long before Christianity, the waxing moon was seen as favorable for planting new crops and starting a new business, for success and making money, while the waning moon was a sign that business would end.

1   2   3   4   5   6   7   8

What are the phases of the moon?

- Phase 1 – new moon
- Phase 2 – waxing crescent moon
- Phase 3 – first quarter moon
- Phase 4 – waxing gibbous moon
- Phase 5 – full moon
- Phase 6 – waning gibbous moon
- Phase 7 – third quarter moon
- Phase 8 – waning crescent moon

To simplify things, we can divide the month into two phases:
Waxing crescent moon - before the full moon
Waning crescent moon - after the full moon

New Moon

We cannot see the new moon, as it is hidden. People might complain about feeling weak, mental imbalance, and fatigue. During this time, we want to avoid taking on too much or overdoing things. Generally, people are not very responsive and react poorly to requests, which is why it is best to look out for yourself, while not keeping your plate too full.

The new moon is a bad time for advertising – it will go unnoticed. It is not worth preparing any presentations, parties, or loud gatherings. People are feeling constrained, not very social, and sluggish.

This is also a less than ideal time for surgery, as your recovery will be slow, and the likelihood of medical error is high.

It is also difficult to get an accurate diagnosis during the new moon – diseases might seem to be hidden, and doctors might not see the real underlying cause of what ails you.

The new moon is also a bad time for dates, and sexual encounters may be dissatisfying and leave you feeling disappointed. Ancient astrologers did not advise planning a wedding night during the new moon.

Waxing Crescent Moon

It is easy to identify a waxing crescent moon. If you draw an imaginary line between the two "horns", you should see the letter P. The waxing moon is then divided into one and two quarters.

During the first quarter moon, we need to focus on planning – setting goals and thinking of how we will set about achieving them. However, it is still a good idea to hold back a bit and not overdo things. Energy levels are still low, though they are growing along with the moon. It is still a good idea to avoid any medical procedures during this time.

The second quarter is a time for bold, decisive action. Things will come easy, and there is a greater chance of a lucky break. This is a good time for weddings, especially if the moon will be in Libra, Cancer, or Taurus. Nevertheless, it is a good idea to put off any advertising activities and public speaking until closer to the full moon, if you can.

Full Moon

During the full moon, the Earth is located between the sun and the moon. During this time, the moon is round and fully illuminated. This takes place during days 14-16 of the lunar cycle.

During the full moon, many people feel more vigorous than usual. They are emotional, sociable, and actively seeking more contact, so this may be a good time for any celebrations.

However, be careful not to drink too much – you can relax to the point that you lose control, and the consequences of that can be very unpleasant. If you are able to stick to moderation, there is no better time for a party!

The full moon is also the best time for advertising, as not only will your campaign be widely seen, people will be apt to remember it.

The full moon is also a favorable time for dates, and during this time, people are at their most open, romantic, and willing to tell each other something important that might take their relationship to the next level of trust and understanding.

Moreover, during the full moon, people feel a surge of energy, which may lead to hyperactivity, restlessness, and insomnia.

It will be harder to keep your emotions in check. You might face conflicts with friends, disasters, and accidents. During the full moon, any surgeries are **not a good idea**, as the risk of complications and bleeding is on the rise. Plastic surgery is also a bad idea, as swelling and bruises might be much worse than in another lunar phase. At the same time, the full moon is a good time to get an accurate diagnosis.

During this time, try to limit your calories and liquid intake (especially if you deal with bloating and excess weight), as your body is absorbing both calories and liquids faster during the full moon, and it can be very difficult to get rid of the weight later on.

Waning Crescent Moon

The full moon is over, and a new phase is beginning – the waning moon. This is a quieter time, when all of the jobs you started earlier are being partly or entirely completed (it all depends on the speed and scale).

Surgery will turn out much better if it is performed during the waning moon. Your recovery will be faster, and the likelihood of complications is much lower. If you have any plans to lose weight, the waning moon is the best time to do that. This is also a good time for quitting bad habits, such as smoking or cursing.

The waning moon can also be divided into the third and fourth quarters.

Third quarter - this is a favorable period, and you are able to resolve a lot of problems without conflict. People are calming down and ready to listen and take in information, while still being active. However, this is not the best time to begin any major projects, especially if you are unsure if you will be able to complete them by the start of the new lunar month.

The third quarter is a good time to get married, especially if the moon is in Cancer, Taurus, or Libra.

Fourth quarter – This is the most passive period of the lunar cycle. You are not as strong as usual. Your energy is lagging. You will be tired until reaching a new beginning. The best thing you can do as the lunar cycle comes to an end is to get things in order, and avoid anything that might get in your way at work or in personal relationships. Examine your successes and failures.

Now, let's discuss the lunar days in greater detail. For centuries, people around the world have described the influence of lunar days, and modern astrologers only add to this work, as they compare old texts to modern life.

The 1ˢᵗ lunar day

The first lunar day is extremely important for the rest of the lunar month. This is a much-needed day to carefully plan your activities and lay the groundwork for the rest of the lunar month. Remember that the first lunar day is not a good day for major activities, but rather for sitting down and planning things.

Avoid conflicts on this day, unless you want them to overshadow the rest of the month. Try to see the positive side of things and imagine that the lunar month will bring you good things both at work and in love. The more vividly you can imagine this, the sooner your desires will come to fruition. Perhaps it would be a good idea to jot down plans that will bring you closer to achieving your dreams. This is the best time for both manifesting and making wishes!

This is also a favorable day when it comes to seeking a new job or starting an academic program.

It is fine to go out on a date on the first lunar day, but limit any sexual contact, as your energy levels are low, and you are likely to end up disappointed.

Getting married on the first lunar day is not recommended.

Avoid getting a haircut – there are many indications that cutting your hair on the first lunar day will have a negative effect on your health and life expectancy.

Under no circumstances should you undergo any major cosmetic procedures, including plastic surgery. Energy levels are low, your skin is dull and almost stagnant. The results will not live up to your expectations, and in the worst-case scenario, you will end up looking worse than before. It is common for cosmetic procedures performed on this day to be disappointing or even useless. Even the best surgeons are less capable.

Your good dreams on the first lunar day foretell happiness and joy. Bad ones usually do not come true.

The 2nd lunar day

This is considered a lucky day, and is symbolized by a cornucopia. It is not an exaggeration to say that the second lunar day is a favorable time for both work and love. It is a time for action, and a great period to work on yourself, look for a new job, start something new, or complete any financial transaction, whether a sale or purchase. This is also a great time for creative and scientific insights, and a good time for any meeting – whether political or romantic.

Any romantic dates or sexual encounters during the second lunar day are unlikely to disappoint. This is also a good day for weddings or taking a trip with someone special.

During the second lunar day, the moon is beginning its waxing phase, which is a good time for anything you might to do nourish and restore your skin. This is a great time for any cosmetic procedures aimed at preservation, though it is best to put off any plastic surgery until the waning moon. If that is not possible, then the second lunar day is acceptable, if not ideal, and you will not run into any complications.

Folklore tells us that this is not a good day for a haircut, as that may lead to arguments with a loved one.

This is the best time for exercise – your body is in good shape, and you are able to handle new exercise regimens. If the moon happens to be in Scorpio, though, be careful.

This is a good day for anything positive, but avoid any conflicts, discussions about the status of your relationship, or litigation.

Dreams of the second lunar day are usually not prophetic.

The 3rd lunar day

On this day, we are usually able to make out a thin sliver of the lunar crescent. It is a longstanding tradition to show money during the new month – it is believed that as the moon grows, so will your savings.

However, astrological systems around the world consider this an unlucky, unfavorable day. It is not a good idea to travel, begin any new business, or give into your bad mood.

You might run into many a lot of problems at work on this day, which will cause you a lot of anxiety. However, it is a good day to take a step back and identify and set about fixing any flaws and shortcomings. Remember that everything tends to look worse on this day than it actually is.

It is not the time to ask management for anything – you are likely to walk away disappointed, and end up unfairly reprimanded rather than receiving a promotion or raise. Instead, focus on areas of work that need to be smoothed over or studied further. It will be clear what problems you are facing, and you will easily be able to find a remedy.

Do not rush to criticize your loved ones – things may not be as they appear. "Measure twice and cut once" is your motto on this day.

This is not a good day to get married, as the couple is likely to have a turbulent, short-lived marriage.

You can schedule a cosmetic procedure for this day, but only if it is relatively minor. Plastic surgery should wait.

Do exercises as usual, without overdoing it or adding any new routines.

Dreams on this day do not mean anything.

The 4th lunar day

These are relatively neutral days, in that they are unlikely to bring anything bad, but they also will not bring you any windfalls. The fourth lunar day is symbolized by a tree of paradise, the tree of knowledge, and the choice between good and evil. Things ultimately depend on us and our final decisions.

This is a great day for anything money-related – signing contracts, agreements, or even taking on credit. There are also a lot of contradictions on this day – on one hand, we are likely to receive money, which is a good thing, but on the other, we will have to give some of it away, which is never particularly fun or pleasant. There is good reason to consider all of your opportunities and possibilities before acting.

It is not a good day to get married, as the wedding will not be as fun as you had hoped. However, the fourth lunar day is, in fact, a good day for sex and conceiving a healthy child.

Be careful on this day if you happen to engage in any physical exercise, as it is not a good idea to overeat or abuse alcohol. Take care of yourself. Any illnesses which began on this day may be extremely dangerous, if they are not dealt with immediately.

Cosmetic procedures are not contraindicated, as long as they are to preserve your appearance. Plastic surgery can be performed if you truly feel it is necessary.

However, avoid getting a haircut, as it is unlikely to grow back healthily, and will become brittle and dull. However, if the moon is in Leo, you can disregard this advice.

Dreams may turn out to be real.

The 5th lunar day

Traditionally, the fifth lunar day is one of the worst of the lunar month. It is symbolized by a unicorn. Unicorns need to be tamed, but only a virgin is capable of doing so. Many people will feel drained on this day, or frustrated with themselves, those around them, and life in general.

Try to avoid arguments- any conflicts are likely to drag out for a long time, and then you may be overcome with guilt. This advice is relevant for both work and love.

Sexual encounters may be pleasant, but this is not a good day to plan a wedding, as it is likely to lead to a marriage full of unpleasant incidents.

Do not start any new businesses, or ask those around you for favors- you may be misunderstood and rejected.

It is fine to engage in physical exercise, but if you overdo it on this day, you may injure yourself.

Your energy levels are low. Cosmetic procedures may not be effective, and avoid any plastic surgeries.

It is good if you dream something connected with the road, trips or with movement in general. A bad dream might be a sign of a health problem which should be addressed.

The 6th lunar day

The symbol of the sixth lunar day is a cloud and a crane. This is a philosophical combination that suggests that it is not worth rushing things on these days. This is a very positive, lucky day for both work and love. Creative work will be especially successful, as will any attempts at opening a new business in your field.

The sixth lunar day is a good time for resolving any financial matters. There is one limitation, however – do not give anyone a loan, as they may not pay it back. But you can certainly sponsor and support those who are more vulnerable than you.

This day is a good time to go on a trip, whether close to home or far away.

This is also a good day for dates, weddings, and marriage proposals. Remember that energy is more romantic than sexual, so it is better to give the gift of roses and a bottle of champagne than hot, passionate sex.

It is a good idea to get some exercise, but do not overdo things, though you will probably not want to, either.

Cosmetic procedures will be successful, and you can even have plastic surgery performed, so long as the moon is not in Scorpio.

It is still a good idea to avoid getting your hair cut, as you might "cut off" something good in addition to your hair.

It is better to not discuss dreams as they are usually true. Your dreams of this day can remind you of something that needs to be completed as soon as possible.

The 7th lunar day

This is also a favorable lunar day, and it is symbolized by a fighting cock, which is an Avestan deity. Avoid any aggression on this day, and instead work on yourself, spend time at home or in nature. Avoid discussing the status of your relationship with anyone, arguing, or wishing bad things on anyone. Everything will come back to haunt you, remember, silence is golden.

Business negotiations and contracts will be successful. You can find support, sponsors, and people ready to help you in both words and deeds.

Lighten up with your colleagues and subordinates. Pay attention not only to their shortcomings, but also to their skills. This is a good day for reconciliation and creating both political and romantic unions.

The seventh lunar day is good for traveling, no matter how near or far from home.

It is also a favorable time for love and marriage.

Exercise moderately, and any plastic surgeries will go very smoothly, as long as the moon is not in Scorpio.

Dreams of this day may become a reality.

The 8th lunar day

The symbol for this day is a Phoenix, which symbolizes eternal rebirth and renewal, because this day is a great time for changes in all areas of your life. Your energy is likely to be high, and you want to do something new and unusual. This is a good time to look for a new job or begin studying something. Any out-of-the-box thinking is welcome, along with shaking things up a bit in order to improve your life.

However, avoid any financial transactions, as you may incur losses.

Avoid aggression. You can share your opinion by presenting well-founded arguments and facts, instead.

The phoenix rises from the ashes, so this is a good time to be careful with electrical appliances and fire in general. The risk of housefires is high.

Avoid any major financial transactions on the eighth day, as you may end up facing a series of complications. You can pay people their salaries, as this is unlikely to be a large sum.

This is a good day for weddings, but only if you and your future spouse are restless, creative souls and hope to achieve personal development through your marriage.

Any cosmetic procedures and plastic surgeries will go well today, as they are related to rebirth and renewal. Surgeons may find that they are true artists on this day!

You can try to change your hairstyle and get a fashionable haircut on this day.

You can trust your dreams seen on this day.

The 9th lunar day

The ninth lunar day is not particularly auspicious, and is even referred to as "Satan's" day. You may be overcome with doubt, suspicions, even depression and conflicts.

Your self-esteem will suffer, so don't overdo things physically, and avoid overeating or abusing alcohol.

This is a negative day for any business deals, travel, or financial transactions.

This is a particularly bad day for any events, so keep your head down at work and avoid any new initiatives.

It is better to avoid getting married on "Satan's" day, as the marriage will not last very long. Avoid sex, as well, but you can take care of your partner, listen them, and support them however they need.

Any cosmetic procedures will not have a lasting effect, and avoid any plastic surgery. A haircut will not turn out as you hoped.

Dreams of this day are usually prophetic.

The 10th lunar day

This is one of the luckiest days of the lunar month. It is symbolized by a spring, mushroom, or phallus. This is a time for starting a new business, learning new things, and creating.

The 10th lunar day is particularly lucky for business. Networking and financial transactions will be a success and bring hope. This is an ideal time for changing jobs, shifting your business tactics, and other renewals.

This is a perfect time for people in creative fields and those working in science, who may come up with incredible ideas that will bring many successful returns.

This is a very successful day for building a family and proposing marriage. This is a good time for celebrations and communication, so plan parties, meet with friends, and plan a romantic date.

One of the symbols for this day is a phallus, so sexual encounters are likely to be particularly satisfying.

The 10th lunar day is the best time to begin repairs, buying furniture, and items for home improvement.

You can exercise vigorously, and cosmetic procedures and plastic surgery will be very effective.

Dreams of this day will not come true.

The 11th lunar day

This is one of the best lunar days, and seen as the pinnacle of the lunar cycle. People are likely to be energetic, enthusiastic, and ready to move forward toward their goals.

The 11th lunar day is very successful for any financial transactions or business deals and meetings.

You might actively make yourself known, approach management to discuss a promotion, or look for a new job. This is an auspicious time for advertising campaigns, performances, and holding meetings.

Any trips planned will be a great success, whether near or far from home.

Romantic relationships are improving, sex is harmonious, and very desired.

Weddings held on this day will be fun, and the marriage will be a source of joy and happiness.

Exercise is a great idea, and you might even beat your own personal record.

This is an ideal time for any cosmetic procedures, but any more serious plastic surgeries might lead to a lot of bruising and swelling.

A haircut will turn out as you had hoped, and you can experiment a bit with your appearance.

You can ignore dreams of this day – usually they do not mean anything.

The 12th lunar day

This day is symbolized by the Grail and a heart. As we move closer to the full moon, our emotions are at their most open. During this time, if you ask someone for something, your request will be heeded. This is a day of faith, goodness, and divine revelations.

For business and financial transactions, this is not the most promising day. However, if you help others on this day, your good deeds are sure to come back to you.

This is a day for reconciliation, so do not try to explain your relationships, as no one is at fault, and it is better to focus on yourself, anyway.

Avoid weddings and sex on this day, but if you want to do what your partner asks, there is no better time.

Many may feel less than confident and cheerful during this day, so take it easy when working out. Avoid overeating, stay hydrated, and avoid alcohol.

The 12th lunar day is not the best for getting married or having sex, but the stars would welcome affection and a kind word.

Avoid getting a haircut, or any plastic surgeries. This is a neutral day for minor cosmetic procedures.

Nearly all dreams will come true.

The 13th lunar day

This day is symbolized by Samsara, the wheel of fate, which is very erratic and capable of moving in any direction. This is why the 13th lunar day is full of contradictions. In Indian traditions, this day is compared to a snake eating its own tail. This is a day for paying off old debts and returning to unfinished business.

Avoid beginning any new business on this day. It is preferable to finish old tasks and proofread your work. Information you receive on this day may not be reliable and must be verified.

It is worth resolving financial problems very carefully, and avoid arguments and conflict.

Do not change jobs on this day or go to a new place for the first time. Do not sit at home alone, though, go see old friends, parents, or older family members.

Minor cosmetic procedures are welcome on this day, but avoid any plastic surgery, as you may experience major swelling and bruising. Avoid any haircuts, too.

As a rule, all dreams will come true.

The 14th lunar day

It's a full moon! The 14th lunar day is one of the happiest, and it is symbolized by the trumpet. Pay attention – you may run into new, much-needed information. Networking will be successful, and you can confidently sign agreements, meet with people, and attend fun gatherings or other leisure activities. This is one of the best days for advertising, performances, and concerts, and those working in creative professions should keep this in mind, as should those who work in politics. Do not sit in place on this day – you need to get out and see others, make new connections, and try to be visible.

This is one of the best days for communication with and making requests from management, as your initiatives will be noticed and welcome. You might talk about a promotion, raise, or something similarly related to professional growth.

Couples will see their relationship is moving along well on this day, and it is also a good day for getting married.

Any sex on this day will be vigorous and memorable for a long time. The full moon is the best time for conceiving a child.

Any cosmetic procedures will be effective, but avoid any major changes to your appearance, as there is a high likelihood of bleeding and bruising. A haircut will turn out well.

Your dreams of this day will be more or less doubtful.

The 15th lunar day

It's a full moon! This day is symbolized by a serpent of fire. This is the energy peak of the entire lunar cycle, and a lot will depend on where you are focusing your energy.

You might face a lot of temptations on this day, for example, you might tell someone else's secret or your own to others, and come to regret it for a long time. The stars suggest exercising restraint in both your words and actions, as the 15th day of the lunar cycle is a day of deception and weaknesses.

This is a very active time, and many people might take unnecessary risks. This is not the best day for signing any agreements or contracts. For any performances, concerts, or advertising, however, this is one of the best days of the month.

You can get married on the 15th day, but only if you know each other well and have carefully considered your partnership, without any hasty decisions. This is also a favorable day for a second marriage.

Your romantic relationship is looking wonderful – you are on cloud 9, writing poetry, and deeply convinced of how right your partner is for you – and they feel the same way. It is important that this does not suddenly lead to an abrupt disappointment.

Avoid getting any haircuts on the 15th day of the month, as you may end up with a headache.

Conservative cosmetic procedures and creams will be very effective, but avoid any injections or plastic surgery today. Bleeding, swelling, and bruising are all but guaranteed.

Dreams on the 15th day nearly always come true.

The 16th lunar day

This day is symbolized by a dove. The full moon is over, and the moon is now in its waning phase. Usually, after the turbulent days of the full moon, people feel a bit under the weather. They are not cheerful, and want to avoid excess worry and give themselves a chance to breathe.

Don't ignore your body's wishes, take it easy with physical activities, and take some time for yourself. You might spend time in nature, in the forest, or at a country home.

The 16th day of the lunar month is a time for moderation in all areas – your behavior, eating, and even in your clothes. If you overate during the full moon period, now is the time to diet a bit or at least avoid fatty foods and meat.

This is not a promising day for resolving any financial matters. Keep your documents in order and get ready for any future meetings, instead. If you help a loved one, your good deed will come back 100 times over.

Avoid getting married today, as well as sex.

Cosmetic procedures are likely to be a success, especially if they are related to cleansing your skin, but it is best to avoid any plastic surgery or injections. Your body is not ready to accept them. A haircut will turn out as you hoped.

Any dreams are likely to come true, but that also depends on a correct interpretation.

The 17th lunar day

This day is represented by a vine and bell. It is a happy day and both successful and fun-filled. It is also a good time for negotiations, concluding small business deals, shaking up staffing, and creativity. However, you should keep in mind that the 17th day is only favorable for minor business, and you should avoid starting any major events.

Avoid any major financial transactions on this day. Do not give anyone money as a loan or borrow anything yourself, either.

Any travel, whether for business or pleasure, is likely to be a success.

The 17th day is a great time to get married, and an ideal day for dates. Any sexual encounters will bring you happiness and joy.

Avoid getting your hair cut on this day, but cosmetic procedures and plastic surgery will be a success. Women will look better than usual.

Your dreams are likely to come true in three days.

The 18th lunar day

This day is represented by a mirror. It is a difficult, and generally unpromising day, too. Just as the mirror reflects our imperfections back to us, we need to remember that moderation and modesty are key.

The 18th day is not a favorable time for any business meetings or financial transactions. You can, however work on jobs you already began. It is, however, a positive day for those who work in research or the creative fields.

Your motto of the day is to keep a cool head when it comes to your opportunities and the opportunities of those around you. This is relevant for both work and romantic relationships. It is not a good time to criticize others – any conflicts or arguments may lead to lasting consequences, which you do not need.

Avoid getting married on this day, as well as sexual encounters, which are likely to be disappointing. It is a good time to take a trip together, which will only be good for your relationship.

Avoid getting your hair cut, though this is a relatively neutral day for a haircut, which might turn out well, and though it will not exceed your expectations, it will also not leave you upset. Avoid any plastic surgeries.

Dreams on this day will come true.

The 19th lunar day

This is a very difficult day and it is represented by a spider. The energy is complicated, if not outright dangerous. Don't panic or get depressed, though – this is a test of your strength, and if you are able to hold onto all you have achieved. This is relevant for both work and love. On the 19th day, you should avoid taking any trips.

The energy of the 19th lunar day is very unfavorable for beginning any major projects, and business in general. Work on what you started earlier, get your affairs in order, think over your ideas and emotions, and check to make sure that everything you have done hitherto is living up to your expectations. Do not carry out any financial transactions or take out any loans – do not loan anyone else money, either. Do not ask your managers for anything as they are unlikely to listen to what you have to say, and make judgments instead.

This is a day when you might face outright deception, so do not take any risks and ignore rumors. Do not work on anything related to real estate or legal matters.

This is a very hard time for people with an unbalanced psyche, as they may experience sudden exacerbations or even suicidal ideations.

This is a very unlucky day to get married. Sexual encounters might be disappointing and significantly worsen your relationship.

Avoid any haircuts or cosmetic procedures or surgeries.

Your dreams of this day will come true.

The 20th lunar day

This is also a difficult day, though less so than the 19th. It is represented by an eagle. This is a good time to work on your own development and spiritual growth, by speaking to a psychologist or astrologer.

Avoid pride, anger, arrogance, and envy.

The 20th lunar day is a good time for people who are active and decisive. They will be able to easily overcome any obstacles, flying over them just like an eagle. If you have to overcome your own fears, you will be able to do so – don't limit yourself, and you will see that there is nothing to be afraid of. It is a good day for any financial transactions, signing contracts, and reaching agreements, as well as networking.

The 20th lunar day is a favorable time for those who work in the creative fields, as they will be able to dream up the idea that will open up a whole host of new possibilities. Avoid conflicts – they may ruin your relationship with a lot of people, and it will not be easy to come back from that.

This is a lucky day for getting married, but only if you have been with your partner for several years, now. Sexual encounters will not be particularly joyful, but they also will not cause you any problems.

Avoid getting your hair cut, but you can certainly get it styled. The 20th lunar day is a good day for those who are looking to lose weight. You will be able to do so quickly, and it will be easy for you to follow a diet.

Cosmetic procedures will be a success, as will any plastic surgeries.

Pay attention to dreams of this day as they are likely to come true.

The 21st lunar day

This is one of the most successful days of the lunar month, and it is symbolized by a herd of horses – imagine energy, strength, speed, and bravery. Everything you think up will happen quickly, and you will be able to easily overcome obstacles. A mare is not only brave but also an honest animal, so you will only experience this luck if you remember that honesty is always the best policy.

This is also a favorable day for business. Reaching new agreements and signing contracts, or dealing with foreign partners – it is all likely to be a success. Any financial issues will be resolved successfully.

Those in the creative world will be able to show off their talent and be recognized for their work. Anyone involved in the performing arts can expect success, luck, and recognition. A galloping herd of horses moves quickly, so you might transition to a new job, move to a new apartment, or go on a business trip or travel with your better half.

The 21st lunar day is one of the best to get married or have a sexual encounter.

This is a great time for athletes, hunters, and anyone who likes adventurous activities.

But for criminals and thieves, this is not a lucky or happy day – they will quickly be brought to justice.

Any haircuts or cosmetic procedures are likely to be a huge success and bring both beauty and happiness. You will recover quickly after any surgeries, perhaps without any swelling or bruising at all.

Dreams tend to not be reliable.

The 22nd lunar day

This day will be strange and contradictory. It is symbolized by the elephant Ganesha. According to Indian mythology, Ganesha is the patron saint of hidden knowledge. so this is a favorable day for anyone who is trying to learn more about the world and ready to find the truth, though this is often seen as a hopeless endeavor. This is a day for philosophers and wisemen and women. However, it is an inauspicious day for business, and unlikely to lead to resolving financial issues, signing contracts, agreements, or beginning new projects. You can expect trouble at work.

For creative people, and new employees, this is a successful day.

This is a good day for apologies and reconciliation.

Avoid getting married, though you can feel free to engage in sexual encounters.

For haircuts and cosmetic procedures, this is a fantastic day. Surgeries will also turn out, as long as the moon is not in Scorpio.

Dreams will come true.

The 23rd lunar day

This is a challenging day represented by a crocodile, which is a very aggressive animal. This is a day of strong energy, but it is also adventurous and tough. Your main task is to focus your energy in the right direction. There may be accidents, arguments, conflicts, fights, and violence, which is why it is important to strive for balance and calm.

Keep a close eye on your surroundings – there may be traitors or people who do not wish you well, so be careful.

However, this is still a favorable day for business – many problems will be resolved successfully. You are able to sign contracts and receive credit successfully, as long as you remain active and decisive in what you do.

This is not a day for changing jobs or working on real estate transactions or legal proceedings. This is not a favorable day for traveling, no matter how near or far you plan on going.

This is not a promising day to get married – things may end in conflict, if not an all-out brawl.

Sexual relations are not off the table, as long as the couple trusts one another.

Haircuts or cosmetic procedures will not turn out as you had hoped, so avoid them.

Dreams during this lunar day usually mean something opposite of what awaits you, so you can disregard them.

The 24th lunar day

This is a neutral, calm day that is symbolized by a bear. It is favorable for forgiveness and reconciliation.

This is also a good day for learning new things, reading, self-development, and taking time to relax in nature.

This is a great day for any type of financial activity, conferences, academic meetings, and faraway travel.

The 24th lunar day is a good time for love and getting married, as any marriage will be strong and lasting.

Cosmetic procedures and plastic surgery will be a success, and you can expect a speedy recovery.

Avoid getting a haircut on this day, however, as your hair will likely thin and grow back slowly.

Dreams of this lunar day are usually connected with your personal life.

The 25th lunar day

This is still another quiet day, symbolized by a turtle.

Just like a turtle, this is not a day to rush, and it is best to sit down and take stock of your life. This is a good time for resolving any personal problems, as the moon's energy makes it possible for you to calm down and find the right path.

This is also not a bad day for business. It is believed that any business you begin on this day is sure to be a success. This is especially the case for trade and any monetary activities.

The 25th lunar day is not a good day to get married, especially if the couple is very young.

This is a neutral day for sexual encounters, as the moon is waning, energy is low, so the decision is yours.

Avoid any cosmetic procedures, except those for cleansing your skin. This is not a favorable day for haircuts or plastic surgery – unless the moon is in Libra or Leo.

You can have a prophetic dream on this day.

The 26th lunar day

The 26th lunar day is full of contradictions and complicated. It is represented by a toad.

It is not time to start or take on something new, as nothing good will come of it. Avoid any major purchases, as you will later come to see that your money was wasted. The best thing you can do on this day is stay at home and watch a good movie or read a good book.

Avoid traveling on this day, as it may not turn out well.

The 26th lunar day is a negative day for any business negotiations and starting new businesses. Do not complete any business deals or financial transactions. Your colleagues may be arguing, and your managers may be dissatisfied. But if you have decided to leave your job, there is no better time to do so.

This is not a good day to get married, as both partners' expectations may fall flat, and they will soon be disappointed.

The waning moon carries a negative charge, so avoid any haircuts and surgeries, though you can get cosmetic procedures if they are relatively minor.

Your dreams will come true.

The 27th lunar day

The 27th lunar day is one of the best days of the month, and it is represented by a ship. You can boldly start any new business, which is sure to be promising. This is a great day for students, teachers, and learning new things. Any information that comes to you on this day may be extremely valuable and useful to you.

The 27th day is good for communication and travel, whether near or far from home, and no matter whether it is for work or pleasure.

This is also a good day for any professional activities or financial transactions. If there are people around you who need help, you must support them, as your good deeds will come back 100-fold.

Romantic dates will go well, though any weddings should be quiet and subdued. This is a particularly good day for older couples or second marriages.

The waning moon means that hair will grow back very slowly, but in general, you can expect a haircut to turn out well. This is a great day for plastic surgery or cosmetic procedures, as the results will be pleasing, and you will have a speedy recovery, without any bruising or swelling, most of the time.

However, beware if the moon is in Scorpio on this day – that is not a good omen for any plastic surgery.

Do not pay any attention to dreams on this day.

The 28ᵗʰ lunar day

This is another favorable day in the waning moon cycle, and it is represented by a lotus. This is a day of wisdom and spiritual awakening. If possible, spend part of the day in nature. It is important to take stock of the last month and decide what you need to do during its two remaining days.

This is a good time for any career development, changing jobs, conducting business, decision-making, and signing agreements, as well as going on a trip. You might conclude any business deal, hold negotiations, work with money and securities.

This is also a good day for any repairs or improvements around your home or apartment.

Any weddings today should be subdued and modest, and restricted to family members only. A loud, raucous wedding might not turn out very well.

Your hair will grow slowly, but any haircuts will turn out very elegant and stylish. Cosmetic procedures and surgeries are not contraindicated. You will recover quickly with little bruising and swelling.

Do not take any dreams too seriously.

The 29th lunar day

This is one of the most difficult days of the lunar month, and it is considered a Satanic day, unlucky for everyone and everything. It is symbolized by an octopus.

This is a dark day, and many will feel melancholy, depression, and a desire to simply be left alone. This is a day full of conflict and injuries, so be careful everywhere and with everyone. If you can, avoid any travel, and be particularly careful when handling any sharp objects. Do not engage in any business negotiations, sign any contracts, or take part in any networking.

Astrologers believe that anything you start on this day will completely fall apart. For once and for all, get rid of things that are impeding you from living your life. This is a good time to avoid people who you do find unpleasant.

This is also a time for fasting and limitations for everyone. Do not hold any celebrations, weddings, or have sexual relations – these events may not turn out as you hoped, and instead bring you nothing but suffering and strife.

Avoid getting a haircut, as well, as it will not make you look more beautiful and your hair will come back lifeless and dull. Cosmetic procedures can go ahead, but avoid any surgeries.

Dreams are likely to be true.

The 30th lunar day

There is not always a 30th lunar day, as some lunar months have only 29 days. This day is represented by a swan. The 30th lunar day is usually very short, and sometimes, it lasts less than an hour. This is a time for forgiveness and calm.

You might take stock of the last month, while also avoiding anything you do not need around you. Pay back loans, make donations, reconcile with those who recently offended you, and stop speaking to people who cause you suffering.

This is a good time for tying up loose ends, and many astrologers believe that it is also a good day to start new business.

However, avoid celebrations or weddings on this day. Spouses will either not live long, or they will quickly grow apart.

Do not get a haircut on this day, though cosmetic procedures are possible, as long as you avoid any surgeries.

Dreams promise happiness and should come true.

A Guide to Zodiac Compatibility

Often, when we meet a person, we get a feeling that they are good and we take an instant liking to them. Another person, however, gives us immediate feelings of distrust, fear and hostility. Is there an astrological reason why people say that 'the first impression is the most accurate'? How can we detect those who will bring us nothing but trouble and unhappiness?

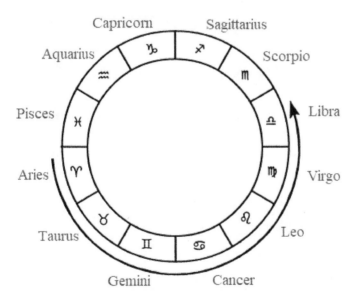

Without going too deeply into astrological subtleties unfamiliar to some readers, it is possible to determine the traits according to which friendship, love or business relationships will develop.

Let's begin with problematic relationships - our most difficult are with our **8th sign**. For example, for Aries the 8th sign is Scorpio, for Taurus it is Sagittarius and so on. Finding your 8th sign is easy; assume your own sign to be first (see above Figure) and then move eight signs counter clockwise around the Zodiac circle. This is also how the other signs (fourth, ninth and so on) that we mention are to be found.

Ancient astrologers variously referred to the 8th sign as the symbol of death, of destruction, of fated love or unfathomable attraction. In astrological terms, this pair is called 'master and slave' or 'boa constrictor and rabbit', with the role of 'master' or 'boa constrictor' being played by our 8th sign.

This relationship is especially difficult for politicians and business people.

We can take the example of a recent political confrontation in the USA. Hilary Clinton is a Scorpio while Donald Trump is a Gemini - her 8th sign. Even though many were certain that Clinton would be elected President, she lost.

To take another example, Hitler was a Taurus and his opponents – Stalin and Churchill - were both of his 8th sign, Sagittarius. The result of their confrontation is well known. Interestingly, the Russian Marshals who dealt crushing military blows to Hitler and so helped end the Third Reich - Konstantin Rokossovsky and Georgy Zhukov - were also Sagittarian, Hitler's 8th sign.

In another historical illustration, Lenin was also a Taurus. Stalin was of Lenin's 8th sign and was ultimately responsible for the downfall and possibly death of his one-time comrade-in-arms.

Business ties with those of our 8th sign are hazardous as they ultimately lead to stress and loss; both financial and moral. So, do not tangle with your 8th sign and never fight with it - your chances of winning are remote!

Such relationships are very interesting in terms of love and romance, however. We are magnetically attracted to our 8th sign and even though it may be very intense physically, it is very difficult for family life; 'Feeling bad when together, feeling worse when apart'.

As an example, let us take the famous lovers - George Sand who was Cancer and Alfred de Musset who was Sagittarius. Cancer is the 8th sign for Sagittarius, and the story of their crazy two-year love affair was the subject of much attention throughout France. Critics and writers were divided into 'Mussulist' and 'Sandist' camps; they debated fiercely about who was to blame for the sad ending to their love story - him or her. It's hard to imagine the energy needed to captivate the public for so long, but that energy was destructive for the couple. Passion raged in their hearts, but neither of them was able to comprehend their situation.

Georges Sand wrote to Musset, "*I ◆on't love you anymore, an◆ I will always a◆ore you. I ◆on't want you anymore, an◆ I can't ◆o without you. It seems that nothing but a heavenly lightning strike can heal me by ◆estroying me. Goo◆-bye! Stay or go, but ◆on't say that I am not suffering. This is the only thing that can make me suffer even more, my love, my life, my bloo◆! Go away, but kill me, leaving.*" Mussent replied only in brief, but its power surpassed Sand's tirade, "*When you embrace◆ me, I felt something that is still bothering me, making it impossible for me to approach another woman.*" These two people loved each other passionately and for two years lived together in a powder keg of passion, hatred and treachery.

When someone enters into a romantic liaison with their 8th sign, there will be no peace; indeed, these relationships are very attractive to those who enjoy the edgy, the borderline and, in the Dostoevsky style, the melodramatic. The first to lose interest in the relationship is, as a rule, the 8th sign.

If, by turn of fate, our child is born under our 8th sign, they will be very different from us and, in some ways, not live up to our expectations. It may be best to let them choose their own path.

In business and political relationships, the combination with our **12th sign** is also a complicated one.

We can take two political examples. Angela Merkel is a Cancer while Donald Trump is a Gemini - her 12th sign. This is why their relations are strained and complicated and we can even perhaps assume that the American president will achieve his political goals at her expense. Boris

Yeltsin (Aquarius) was the 12th sign to Mikhail Gorbachev (Pisces) and it was Yeltsin who managed to dethrone the champion of Perestroika.

Even ancient astrologers noticed that our relationships with our 12th signs can never develop evenly; it is one of the most curious and problematic combinations. They are our hidden enemies and they seem to be digging a hole for us; they ingratiate themselves with us, discover our innermost secrets. As a result, we become bewildered and make mistakes when we deal with them. Among the Roman emperors murdered by members of their entourage, there was an interesting pattern - all the murderers were the 12th sign of the murdered.

We can also see this pernicious effect in Russian history: the German princess Alexandra (Gemini) married the last Russian Tsar Nicholas II (Taurus) - he was her 12th sign and brought her a tragic death. The wicked genius Grigory Rasputin (Cancer) made friends with Tsarina Alexandra, who was his 12th sign, and was murdered as a result of their odd friendship. The weakness of Nicholas II was exposed, and his authority reduced after the death of the economic and social reformer Pyotr Stolypin, who was his 12th sign. Thus, we see a chain of people whose downfall was brought about by their 12th sign.

So, it makes sense to be cautious of your 12th sign, especially if you have business ties. Usually, these people know much more about us than we want them to and they will often reveal our secrets for personal gain if it suits them. However, the outset of these relationships is, as a rule, quite normal - sometimes the two people will be friends, but sooner or later one will betray the other one or divulge a secret; inadvertently or not.

In terms of romantic relationships, our 12th sign is gentle, they take care of us and are tender towards us. They know our weaknesses well but accept them with understanding. It is they who guide us, although sometimes almost imperceptibly. Sexual attraction is usually strong.

For example, Meghan Markle is a Leo, the 12th sign for Prince Harry, who is a Virgo. Despite Queen Elizabeth II being lukewarm about the match, Harry's love was so strong that they did marry.

If a child is our 12th sign, it later becomes clear that they know all our secrets, even those that they are not supposed to know. It is very difficult to control them as they do everything in their own way.

Relations with our **7th sign** are also interesting. They are like our opposite; they have something to learn from us while we, in turn, have something to learn from them. This combination, in business and personal relationships, can be very positive and stimulating provided that both partners are quite intelligent and have high moral standards but if not, constant misunderstandings and challenges follow. Marriage or co-operation with the 7th sign can only exist as the union of two fully-fledged individuals and in this case love, significant business achievements and social success are possible.

However, the combination can be not only interesting, but also quite complicated.

An example is Angelina Jolie, a Gemini, and Brad Pitt, a Sagittarius. This is a typical bond with a 7th sign - it's lively and interesting, but rather stressful. Although such a couple may quarrel and even part from time to time, never do they lose interest in each other.

This may be why this combination is more stable in middle-age when there is an understanding of the true nature of marriage and partnership. In global, political terms, this suggests a state of eternal tension - a cold war - for example between Yeltsin (Aquarius) and Bill Clinton (Leo).

Relations with our **9th sign** are very good; they are our teacher and advisor - one who reveals things we are unaware of and our relationships with them very often involve travel or re-location. The combination can lead to spiritual growth and can be beneficial in terms of business.

Although, for example, Trump and Putin are political opponents, they can come to an understanding and even feel a certain sympathy for each other because Putin is a Libra while Trump is a Gemini, his 9th sign.

This union is also quite harmonious for conjugal and romantic relationships.

We treat our **3rd sign** somewhat condescendingly. They are like our younger siblings; we teach them and expect them to listen attentively. Our younger brothers and sisters are more often than not born under this sign. In terms of personal and sexual relationships, the union is not very inspiring and can end quickly, although this is not always the case. In terms of business, it is fairly average as it often connects partners from different cities or countries.

We treat our **5th sign** as a child and we must take care of them accordingly. The combination is not very good for business, however, since our 5th sign triumphs over us in terms of connections and finances, and thereby gives us very little in return save for love or sympathy. However, they are very good for family and romantic relationships, especially if the 5th sign is female. If a child is born as a 5th sign to their parents, their relationship will be a mutually smooth, loving and understanding one that lasts a lifetime.

Our **10th sign** is a born leader. Depending on the spiritual level of those involved, both pleasant and tense relations are possible; the relationship is often mutually beneficial in the good times but mutually disruptive in the bad times. In family relations, our 10th sign always tries to lead and will do so according to their intelligence and upbringing.

Our **4th sign** protects our home and can act as a sponsor to strengthen our financial or moral positions. Their advice should be heeded in all cases as it can be very effective, albeit very unobtrusive. If a woman takes this role, the relationship can be long and romantic, since all the spouse's wishes are usually met one way or another. Sometimes, such couples achieve great social success; for instance, Hilary Clinton, a Scorpio is the 4th sign to Bill Clinton, a Leo. On the other hand, if the husband is the 4th sign for his wife, he tends to be henpecked. There is often a strong sexual attraction. Our 4th sign can improve our living conditions and care for us in a parental way. If a child is our 4th sign, they are close to us and support us affectionately.

Relations with our **11th sign** are often either friendly or patronizing; we treat them reverently, while they treat us with friendly condescension. Sometimes, these relationships develop in an 'older brother' or 'high-ranking friend' sense; indeed, older brothers and sisters are often our 11th sign. In terms of personal and sexual relationships, our 11th sign is always inclined to enslave us. This tendency is most clearly manifested in such alliances as Capricorn and Pisces or Leo and Libra. A child who is the 11th sign to their parents will achieve greater success than their parents, but this will only make the parents proud.

Our **2nd sign** should bring us financial or other benefits; we receive a lot from them in both our business and our family life. In married couples, the 2nd sign usually looks after the financial situation for the benefit of the family. Sexual attraction is strong.

Our **6th sign** is our 'slave'; we always benefit from working with them and it's very difficult for them to escape our influence. In the event of hostility, especially if they have provoked the conflict, they receive a powerful retaliatory strike. In personal relations, we can almost destroy them by making them dance to our tune. For example, if a husband doesn't allow his wife to work or there are other adverse family circumstances, she gradually becomes lost as an individual despite being surrounded by care. This is the best-case scenario; worse outcomes are possible. Our 6th sign has a strong sexual attraction to us because we are the fatal 8th sign for them; we cool down quickly, however, and often make all kinds of demands. If the relationship with our 6th sign is a long one, there is a danger that routine, boredom and stagnation will ultimately destroy the relationship. A child born under our 6th sign needs particularly careful handling as they can feel fear or embarrassment when communicating with us. Their health often needs increased attention and we should also remember that they are very different from us emotionally.

Finally, we turn to relations with **our own sign**. Scorpio with Scorpio and Cancer with Cancer get along well, but in most other cases, however, our own sign is of little interest to us as it has a similar energy. Sometimes, this relationship can develop as a rivalry, either in business or in love.

There is another interesting detail - we are often attracted to one particular sign. For example, a man's wife and mistress often have the same sign. If there is confrontation between the two, the stronger character displaces the weaker one. As an example, Prince Charles is a Scorpio, while both Princess Diana and Camilla Parker Bowles were born under the sign of Cancer. Camilla was the more assertive and became dominant.

Of course, in order to draw any definitive conclusions, we need an individually prepared horoscope, but the above always, one way or another, manifests itself.

Love Description of Zodiac Signs

We know that human sexual behavior has been studied at length. Entire libraries have been written about it, with the aim of helping us understand ourselves and our partners. But is that even possible? It may not be; no matter how smart we are, when it comes to love and sex, there is always an infinite amount to learn. But we have to strive for perfection, and astrology, with its millennia of research, twelve astrological types, and twelve zodiac signs, may hold the key. Below, you will find a brief and accurate description of each zodiac sign's characteristics in love, for both men and women.

Men

ARIES

Aries men are not particularly deep or wise, but they make up for it in sincerity and loyalty. They are active, even aggressive lovers, but a hopeless romantic may be lurking just below the surface. Aries are often monogamous and chivalrous men, for whom there is only one woman (of course, in her absence, they can sleep around with no remorse). If the object of your affection is an Aries, be sure to give him a lot of sex, and remember that for an Aries, when it comes to sex, anything goes. Aries cannot stand women who are negative or disheveled. They need someone energetic, lively, and to feel exciting feelings of romance.

The best partner for an Aries is Cancer, Sagittarius, or Leo. Aquarius can also be a good match, but the relationship will be rather friendly in nature. Partnering with a Scorpio or Taurus will be difficult, but they can be stimulating lovers for an Aries. Virgos are good business contacts, but a poor match as lovers or spouses.

TAURUS

A typical Taurean man is warm, friendly, gentle, and passionate, even if he doesn't always show it. He is utterly captivated by the beauty of the female body, and can find inspiration in any woman. A Taurus has such excess physical and sexual prowess, that to him, sex is a way to relax and calm down. He is the most passionate and emotional lover of the Zodiac, but he expects his partner to take the initiative, and if she doesn't, he will easily find someone else. Taureans rarely divorce, and are true to the end – if not sexually, at least spiritually. They are secretive, keep their cards close, and may have secret lovers. If a Taurus does not feel a deep emotional connection with someone, he won't be shy to ask her friends for their number. He prefers a voluptuous figure over an athletic or skinny woman.

The best partners for a Taurus are Cancer, Virgo, Pisces, or Scorpio. Sagittarius can show a Taurus real delights in both body and spirit, but they are unlikely to make it down the aisle. They can have an interesting relationship with an Aquarius – these signs are very different, but sometimes can spend their lives together. They might initially feel attracted to an Aries, before rejecting her.

GEMINI

The typical Gemini man is easygoing and polite. He is calm, collected, and analytical. For a Gemini, passion is closely linked to intellect, to the point that they will try to find an explanation for their actions before carrying them out. But passion cannot be explained, which scares a Gemini, and they begin jumping from one extreme to the other. This is why you will find more bigamists among Geminis than any other sign of the Zodiac. Sometimes, Gemini men even have two families, or divorce and marry several times throughout the course of their lives. This may be because they simply can't let new and interesting experiences pass them by. A Gemini's wife or lover needs to be smart, quick, and always looking ahead. If she isn't, he will find a new object for his affection.

Aquarians, Libras, and Aries make good partners for a Gemini. A Sagittarius can be fascinating for him, but they will not marry before he reaches middle age, as both partners will be fickle while they are younger. A Gemini and Scorpio are likely to be a difficult match, and the Gemini will try to wriggle out of the Scorpio's tight embrace. A Taurus will be an exciting sex partner, but their partnership won't be for long, and the Taurus is often at fault.

CANCER

Cancers tend to be deep, emotional individuals, who are both sensitive and highly sexual. Their charm is almost mystical, and they know how to use it. Cancers may be the most promiscuous sign of the Zodiac, and open to absolutely anything in bed. Younger Cancers look for women who are more mature, as they are skilled lovers. As they age, they look for someone young enough to be their own daughter, and delight in taking on the role of a teacher. Cancers are devoted to building a family and an inviting home, but once they achieve that goal, they are likely to have a wandering eye. They will not seek moral justification, as they sincerely believe it is simply something everyone does. Their charm works in such a way that women are deeply convinced they are the most important love in a Cancer's life, and that circumstances are the only thing preventing them from being together. Remember that a Cancer man is a master manipulator, and will not be yours unless he is sure you have throngs of admirers. He loves feminine curves, and is turned on by exquisite fragrances. Cancers don't end things with old lovers, and often go back for a visit after a breakup. Another type of Cancer is rarer – a faithful friend, and up for anything in order to provide for his wife and children. He is patriotic and a responsible worker.

Scorpios, Pisces, and other Cancers are a good match. A Taurus can make for a lasting relationship, as both signs place great value on family and are able to get along with one another. A Sagittarius will result in fights and blowouts from the very beginning, followed by conflicts and breakups. The Sagittarius will suffer the most. Marriage to an Aries isn't off the table, but it won't last very long.

LEO

A typical Leo is handsome, proud, and vain, with a need to be the center of attention at all times. They often pretend to be virtuous, until they are able to actually master it. They crave flattery, and prefer women who comply and cater to them. Leos demand unconditional obedience, and constant approval. When a Leo is in love, he is fairly sexual, and capable of being devoted and faithful. Cheap love affairs are not his thing, and Leos are highly aware of how expensive it is to divorce. They make excellent fathers. A Leo's partner needs to look polished and well-dressed, and he will not tolerate either frumpiness or nerds.

Aries, Sagittarius, and Gemini make for good matches. Leos are often very beguiling to Libras; this is the most infamous astrological "master-slave" pairing. Leos are also inexplicably drawn to Pisces – this is the only sign capable of taming them. A Leo and Virgo will face a host of problems sooner or later, and they might be material in nature. The Virgo will attempt to conquer him, and if she does, a breakup is inevitable.

VIRGO

Virgo is a highly intellectual sign, who likes to take a step back and spend his time studying the big picture. But love inherently does not lend itself to analysis, and this can leave Virgos feeling perplexed. While Virgo is taking his time, studying the object of his affection, someone else will swoop in and take her away, leaving him bitterly disappointed. Perhaps for that reason, Virgos tend to marry late, but once they are married, they remain true, and hardly ever initiate divorce. In bed, they are modest and reserved, as they see sex as some sort of quirk of nature, designed solely for procreation. Most Virgos have a gifted sense of taste, hearing, and smell. They cannot tolerate pungent odors and can be squeamish; they believe their partners should always take pains to be very clean. Virgos usually hate over-the-top expressions of love, and are immune to sex as a mean s of control. Many Virgos are stingy and more appropriate as husbands than lovers. Male Virgos tend to be monogamous, though if they are unhappy or disappointed with their partner, they may begin to look for comfort elsewhere and often give in to drunkenness.

Taurus, Capricorn, and Scorpio make the best partners for a Virgo. They may feel inexplicable attraction for Aquarians. They will form friendships with Aries, but rarely will this couple make it down the aisle. With Leos, be careful – this sign is best as a lover, not a spouse.

LIBRA

Libra is a very complex, wishy-washy sign. They are constantly seeking perfection, which often leaves them in discord with the reality around them. Libra men are elegant and refined, and expect no less from their partner. Many Libras treat their partners like a beautiful work of art, and have trouble holding onto the object of their affection. They view love itself as a very abstract concept, and can get tired of the physical aspect of their relationship. They are much more drawn to intrigue and the chase- dreams, candlelit evenings, and other symbols of romance. A high percentage of Libra men are gay, and they view sex with other men as the more elite option. Even when Libras are unhappy in their marriages, they never divorce willingly. Their wives might leave them, however, or they might be taken away by a more decisive partner.

Aquarius and Gemini make the best matches for Libras. Libra can also easily control an independent Sagittarius, and can easily fall under the influence of a powerful and determined Leo, before putting all his strength and effort into breaking free. Relationships with Scorpios are difficult; they may become lovers, but will rarely marry.

SCORPIO

Though it is common to perceive Scorpios as incredibly sexual, they are, in fact, very unassuming, and never brag about their exploits. They will, however, be faithful and devoted to the right woman. The Scorpio man is taciturn, and you can't expect any tender words from him, but he will defend those he loves to the very end. Despite his outward control, Scorpio is very emotional; he needs and craves love, and is willing to fight for it. Scorpios are incredible lovers, and rather than leaving them tired, sex leaves them feeling energized. They are always sexy, even if they aren't particularly handsome. They are unconcerned with the ceremony of wooing you, and more focused on the act of love itself.

Expressive Cancers and gentle, amenable Pisces make the best partners. A Scorpio might also fall under the spell of a Virgo, who is adept at taking the lead. Sparks might fly between two Scorpios, or with a Taurus, who is perfect for a Scorpio in bed. Relationships with Libras, Sagittarians, and Aries are difficult.

SAGITTARIUS

Sagittarian men are lucky, curious, and gregarious. Younger Sagittarians are romantic, passionate, and burning with desire to experience every type of love. Sagittarius is a very idealistic sign, and in that search for perfection, they tend to flit from one partner to another, eventually forgetting what they were even looking for in the first place. A negative Sagittarius might have two or three relationships going on at once, assigning each partner a different day of the week. On the other hand, a positive Sagittarius will channel his powerful sexual energy into creativity, and take his career to new heights. Generally speaking, after multiple relationships and divorces, the Sagittarian man will conclude that his ideal marriage is one where his partner is willing to look the other way.

Aries and Leo make the best matches for a Sagittarius. He might fall under the spell of a Cancer, but would not be happy being married to her. Gemini can be very intriguing, but will only make for a happy marriage after middle age, when both partners are older and wiser. Younger Sagittarians often marry Aquarian women, but things quickly fall apart. Scorpios can make for an interesting relationship, but if the Sagittarius fails to comply, divorce is inevitable.

CAPRICORN

Practical, reserved Capricorn is one of the least sexual signs of the Zodiac. He views sex as an idle way to pass the time, and something he can live without, until he wants to start a family. He tends to marry late, and almost never divorces. Young Capricorns are prone to suppressing their sexual desires, and only discover them later in life, when they have already achieved everything a real man needs – a career and money. We'll be frank – Capricorn is not the best lover, but he can compensate by being caring, attentive, and showering you with valuable gifts. Ever cautious, Capricorn loves to schedule his sexual relationships, and this is something partners will just have to accept. Women should understand that Capricorn needs some help relaxing – perhaps with alcohol. They prefer inconspicuous, unassuming women, and run away from a fashion plate.

The best partners for a Capricorn are Virgo, Taurus, or Scorpio. Cancers might catch his attention, and if they marry, it is likely to be for life. Capricorn is able to easily dominate Pisces, and Pisces-Capricorn is a well-known "slave and master" combination. Relationships with Leos tend to be erratic, and they are unlikely to wed. Aries might make for a cozy family at first, but things will cool off quickly, and often, the marriage only lasts as long as Capricorn is unwilling to make a change in his life.

AQUARIUS

Aquarian men are mercurial, and often come off as peculiar, unusual, or aloof, and detached. Aquarians are turned on by anything novel or strange, and they are constantly looking for new and interesting people. They are stimulated by having a variety of sexual partners, but they consider this to simply be normal life, rather than sexually immoral. Aquarians are unique – they are more abstract than realistic, and can be cold and incomprehensible, even in close relationships. Once an Aquarius gets married, he will try to remain within the realm of decency, but often fails. An Aquarian's partners need uncommon patience, as nothing they do can restrain him. Occasionally, one might encounter another kind of Aquarius – a responsible, hard worker, and exemplary family man.

The best matches for an Aquarius are female fellow Aquarians, Libras, and Sagittarians. When Aquarius seeks out yet another affair, he is not choosy, and will be happy with anyone.

PISCES

Pisces is the most eccentric sign of the Zodiac. This is reflected in his romantic tendencies and sex life. Pisces men become very dependent on those with whom they have a close relationship. Paradoxically, they are simultaneously crafty and childlike when it comes to playing games, and they are easily deceived. As a double bodied sign, Pisces rarely marry just once, as they are very sexual, easily fall in love, and are constantly seeking their ideal. Pisces are very warm people, who love to take care of others and are inclined toward "slave-master" relationships, in which they are the submissive partner. But after catering to so many lovers, Pisces will remain elusive. They are impossible to figure out ahead of time – today, they might be declaring their love for you, but tomorrow, they may disappear – possibly forever! To a Pisces, love is a fantasy, illusion, and dream, and they might spend their whole lives in pursuit of it. Pisces who are unhappy in love are vulnerable to alcoholism or drug addiction.

Cancer and Scorpio make the best partners for a Pisces. He is also easily dominated by Capricorn and Libra, but in turn will conquer even a queen-like Leo. Often, they are fascinated by Geminis – if they marry, it will last a long time, but likely not forever. Relationships with Aries and Sagittarians are erratic, though initially, things can seem almost perfect.

Women

ARIES

Aries women are leaders. They are decisive, bold, and very protective. An Aries can take initiative and is not afraid to make the first move. Her ideal man is strong, and someone she can admire. But remember, at the slightest whiff of weakness, she will knock him off his pedestal. She does not like dull, whiny men, and thinks that there is always a way out of any situation. If she loves someone, she will be faithful. Aries women are too honest to try leading a double life. They are possessive, jealous, and not only will they not forgive those who are unfaithful, their revenge may be brutal; they know no limits. If you can handle an Aries, don't try to put her in a cage; it is best to give her a long leash. Periodically give her some space – then she will seek you out herself. She is sexual, and believe that anything goes in bed.

Her best partners are a Sagittarius or Leo. A Libra can make a good match after middle age, once both partners have grown wiser and settled down a bit. Gemini and Aquarius are only good partners during the initial phase, when everything is still new, but soon enough, they will lose interest in each other. Scorpios are good matches in bed, but only suitable as lovers.

TAURUS

Taurean women possess qualities that men often dream about, but rarely find in the flesh – they are soft, charming, practical, and reliable – they are very caring and will support their partner in every way. A Taurus is highly sexual, affectionate, and can show a man how to take pleasure to new heights. She is also strong and intense. If she is in love, she will be faithful. But when love fades away, she might find someone else on the side, though she will still fight to save her marriage, particularly if her husband earns good money. A Taurus will not tolerate a man who is disheveled or disorganized, and anyone dating her needs to always be on his toes. She will expect gifts, and likes being taken to expensive restaurants, concerts, and other events. If you argue, try to make the first peace offering, because a Taurus finds it very hard to do so – she might withdraw and ruminate for a long time. Never air your dirty laundry; solve all your problems one-on-one.

Scorpio, Virgo, Capricorn, and Cancer make the best matches. A relationship with an Aries or Sagittarius would be difficult. There is little attraction between a Taurus and a Leo, and initially Libras can make for a good partner in bed, but things will quickly cool off and fall apart. A Taurus and Aquarius make an interesting match – despite the difference in signs, their relationships are often lasting, and almost lifelong.

GEMINI

Gemini women are social butterflies, outgoing, and they easily make friends, and then break off the friendship, if people do not hold their interest. A Gemini falls in love hard, is very creative, and often fantasizes about the object of her affection. She is uninterested in sex without any attachment, loves to flirt, and, for the most part, is not particularly affectionate. She dreams of a partner who is her friend, lover, and a romantic, all at once. A Gemini has no use for a man who brings nothing to the table intellectually. That is a tall order, so Geminis often divorce and marry several times. Others simply marry later in life. Once you have begun a life together, do not try to keep her inside – she needs to travel, explore, socialize, attend events and go to the theater. She cannot tolerate possessive men, so avoid giving her the third degree, and remember that despite her flirtatious and social nature, she is, in fact, faithful – as long as you keep her interested and she is in love. Astrologists believe that Geminis do not know what they need until age 29 or 30, so it is best to hold off on marriage until then.

Leo and Libra make the best matches. A relationship with a Cancer is likely, though complex, and depends solely on the Cancer's affection. A Gemini and Sagittarius can have an interesting, dynamic relationship, but these are two restless signs, which might only manage to get together after ages 40-45, once they have had enough thrills out of life and learned to be patient. Relationships with a Capricorn are very difficult, and almost never happen. The honeymoon stage can be wonderful with a Scorpio, but each partner will eventually go their own way, before ending things. A Gemini and Pisces union can also be very interesting – they are drawn to each other, and can have a wonderful relationship, but after a while, the cracks start to show and things will fall apart. An Aquarius is also not a bad match, but they will have little sexual chemistry.

CANCER

Cancers can be divided into two opposing groups. The first includes a sweet and gentle creature who is willing to dedicate her life to her husband and children. She is endlessly devoted to her husband, especially if he makes a decent living and remains faithful. She views all men as potential husbands, which means it is dangerous to strike up a relationship with her if your intentions are not serious; she can be anxious and clingy, sensitive and prone to crying. It is better to break things to her gently, rather than directly spitting out the cold, hard truth. She wants a man who can be a provider, though she often earns well herself. She puts money away for a rainy day, and knows how to be thrifty, for the sake of others around her, rather than only for herself. She is an excellent cook and capable of building an inviting home for her loved ones. She is enthusiastic in bed, a wonderful wife, and a caring mother.

The second type of Cancer is neurotic, and capable of creating a living hell for those around her. She believes that the world is her enemy, and manages to constantly find new intrigue and machinations.

Another Cancer, Virgo, Taurus, Scorpio, and Pisces make the best matches. A Cancer can often fall in love with a Gemini, but eventually, things will grow complicated, as she will be exhausted by a Gemini's constant mood swings and cheating. A Cancer and Sagittarius will initially have passionate sex, but things will quickly cool off. A relationship with a Capricorn is a real possibility, but only later in life, as while they are young, they are likely to fight and argue constantly. Cancer can also have a relationship with an Aries, but this will not be easy.

LEO

Leos are usually beautiful or charming, and outwardly sexual. And yet, appearances can be deceiving – they are not actually that interested in sex. Leo women want to be the center of attention and men running after them boosts their self-esteem, but they are more interested in their career, creating something new, and success than sex. They often have high-powered careers and are proud of their own achievements. Their partners need to be strong; if a Leo feels a man is weak, she can carry him herself for a while- before leaving him. It is difficult for her to find a partner for life, as chivalrous knights are a dying breed, and she is not willing to compromise. If you are interested in a Leo, take the initiative, admire her, and remember that even a queen is still a woman. Timid men or tightwads need not apply. Leos like to help others, but they don't need a walking disaster in their life. If they are married and in love, they are usually faithful, and petty gossip isn't their thing. Leo women make excellent mothers, and are ready to give their lives to their children. Their negative traits include vanity and a willingness to lie, in order to make themselves look better.

Sagittarius, Aries, and Libra make the best matches. Leos can also have an interesting relationship with a Virgo, though both partners will weaken each other. Life with a Taurus will lead to endless arguments – both signs are very stubborn, and unwilling to give in. Leos and Pisces are another difficult pair, as she will have to learn to be submissive if she wants to keep him around. A relationship with a Capricorn will work if there is a common denominator, but they will have little sexual chemistry. Life with a Scorpio will be turbulent to say the least, and they will usually break up later in life.

VIRGO

Virgo women are practical, clever, and often duplicitous. Marrying one isn't for everyone. She is a neat freak to the point of annoying those around her. She is also an excellent cook, and strives to ensure her children receive the very best by teaching them everything, and preparing them for a bright future. She is also thrifty – she won't throw money around, and, in fact, won't even give it to her husband. She has no time for rude, macho strongmen, and is suspicious of spendthrifts. She will not be offended if you take her to a cozy and modest café rather than an elegant restaurant. Virgos are masters of intrigue, and manage to outperform every other sign of the Zodiac in this regard. Virgos love to criticize everyone and everything; to listen to them, the entire world is simply a disaster and wrong, and only she is the exception to this rule. Virgos are not believed to be particularly sexual, but there are different variations when it comes to this. Rarely, one finds an open-minded Virgo willing to try anything, and who does it all on a grand scale – but she is rather the exception to this general rule.

The best matches for a Virgo are Cancer, Taurus, and Capricorn. She also can get along well with a Scorpio, but will find conflict with Sagittarius. A Pisces will strike her interest, but they will rarely make it down the aisle. She is often attracted to an Aquarius, but they would drive each other up the wall were they to actually marry. An Aries forces Virgo to see another side of life, but here, she will have to learn to conform and adapt.

LIBRA

Female Libras tend to be beautiful, glamorous, or very charming. They are practical, tactical, rational, though they are adept at hiding these qualities behind their romantic and elegant appearance. Libras are drawn to marriage, and are good at imagining the kind of partner they need. They seek out strong, well-off men and are often more interested in someone's social status and bank account than feelings. The object of their affection needs to be dashing, and have a good reputation in society. Libras love expensive things, jewelry, and finery. If they are feeling down, a beautiful gift will instantly cheer them up. They will not tolerate scandal or conflict, and will spend all their energy trying to keep the peace, or at least the appearance thereof. They do not like to air their dirty laundry, and will only divorce in extreme circumstances. They are always convinced they are right and react to any objections as though they have been insulted. Most Libras are not particularly sexual, except those with Venus or the Moon in Scorpio.

Leos, Geminis, and Aquarians make good matches. Libra women are highly attracted to Aries men - this is a real case of opposites attract. They can get along with a Sagittarius, though he will find that Libras are too proper and calm. Capricorn, Pisces, and Cancer are all difficult matches. Things will begin tumultuously with a Taurus, before each partner goes his or her own way.

SCORPIO

Scorpio women may appear outwardly restrained, but there is much more bubbling below the surface. They are ambitious with high self-esteem, but often wear a mask of unpretentiousness. They are the true power behind the scenes, the one who holds the family together, but never talk about it. Scorpios are strong-willed, resilient, and natural survivors. Often, Scorpios are brutally honest, and expect the same out of those around them. They do not like having to conform, and attempt to get others to adapt to them, as they honestly believe everyone will be better off that way. They are incredibly intuitive, and not easily deceived. They have an excellent memory, and can quickly figure out which of your buttons to push. They are passionate in bed, and their temperament will not diminish with age. When she is sexually frustrated, a Scorpio will throw all of her energy into her career or her loved ones. She is proud, categorical, and "if you don't do it right, don't do it at all" is her motto. Scorpio cannot be fooled, and she will not forgive any cheating. Will she cheat herself? Yes! But it will not break up her family, and she will attempt to keep it a secret. Scorpios are usually attractive to men, even if they are not particularly beautiful. They keep a low profile, though they always figure out their partner, and give them some invisible sign. There is also another, selfish type of Scorpio, who will use others for as long as they need them, before unceremoniously casting them aside.

Taurus is a good match; they will have excellent sexual chemistry and understand each other. Scorpio and Gemini are drawn to each other, but are unlikely to stay together long enough to actually get married. Cancer can be a good partner as well, but Cancers are possessive, while Scorpios do not like others meddling in their affairs, though they can later resolve their arguments in bed. Scorpio and Leo are often found together, but their relationship can also be very complicated. Leos are animated and chipper, while Scorpios, who are much deeper and more stubborn, see Leos as not particularly serious or reliable. One good example of this is Bill (a Leo) and Hillary (a Scorpio) Clinton. Virgo can also make a good partner, but when Scorpio seemingly lacks emotions, he will look for them elsewhere. Relationships with Lira are strange and very rare. Scorpio sees Libra as too insecure, and Libra does not appreciate Scorpio's rigidity. Two Scorpios together make an excellent marriage! Sagittarius and Scorpio are unlikely to get together, as she will think he is shallow and rude. If they do manage to get married, Scorpio's drive and persistence is the only thing that will make the marriage last. Capricorn is also not a bad match, and while Scorpio finds Aquarius attractive, they will rarely get married, as they are simply speaking different languages! Things are alright with a Pisces, as both signs are emotional, and Pisces can let Scorpio take the lead when necessary.

SAGITTARIUS

Sagittarius women are usually charming, bubbly, energetic, and have the gift of gab. They are kind, sincere, and love people. They are also straightforward, fair, and very ambitious, occasionally to the point of irritating those around them. But telling them something is easier than not telling them, and they often manage to win over their enemies. Sagittarius tends to have excellent intuition, and she loves to both learn and teach others. She is a natural leader, and loves taking charge at work and at home. Many Sagittarian women have itchy feet, and prefer all kinds of travel to sitting at home. They are not particularly good housewives – to be frank, cooking and cleaning is simply not for them. Their loved ones must learn to adapt to them, but Sagittarians themselves hate any pressure. They are not easy for men to handle, as Sagittarians want to be in charge. Sagittarius falls in love easily, is very sexual and temperamental, and may marry multiple times. Despite outward appearances, Sagittarius is a very lonely sign. Even after she is married with children, she may continue living as if she were alone;

you might say she marches to the beat of her own drum. Younger Sagittarians can be reckless, but as they mature, they can be drawn to religion, philosophy, and the occult.

Aries and Leo make the best matches, as Sagittarius is able to bend to Leo's ways, or at least pretend to. Sagittarians often end up with Aquarians, but their marriages do not tend to be for the long haul. They are attracted to Geminis, but are unlikely to marry one until middle age, when both signs have settled down. Sagittarius and Cancer have incredible sexual chemistry, but an actual relationship between them would be tumultuous and difficult. Capricorn can make a good partner- as long as they are able to respect each other's quirks. Sagittarius rarely ends up with a Virgo, and while she may often meet Pisces, things are unlikely to go very far.

CAPRICORN

Capricorn women are conscientious, reliable, organized, and hard-working. Many believe that life means nothing but work, and live accordingly. They are practical, and not particularly drawn to parties or loud groups of people. But if someone useful will be there, they are sure to make an appearance. Capricorn women are stingy, but not as much as their male counterparts. They are critical of others, but think highly of themselves. Generally, they take a difficult path in life, but thanks to their dedication, perseverance, and willingness to push their own limits, they are able to forge their own path, and by 45 or 50, they can provide themselves with anything they could want. Capricorn women have the peculiarity of looking older than their peers when they are young, and younger than everyone else once they have matured. They are not particularly sexual, and tend to be faithful partners. They rarely divorce, and even will fight until the end, even for a failed marriage. Many Capricorns have a pessimistic outlook of life, and have a tendency to be depressed. They are rarely at the center of any social circle, but are excellent organizers. They have a very rigid view of life and love, and are not interested in a fling, as marriage is the end goal. As a wife, Capricorn is simultaneously difficult and reliable. She is difficult because of her strict nature and difficulty adapting. But she will also take on all the household duties, and her husband can relax, knowing his children are in good hands.

Taurus, Pisces, and Scorpio make good matches. Aries is difficult, once things cool off after the initial honeymoon. When a Capricorn meets another Capricorn, they will be each other's first and last love. Sagittarius isn't a bad match, but they don't always pass the test of time. Aquarius and Capricorn are a difficult match, and rarely found together. Things are too dull with a Virgo, and while Leo can be exciting at first, things will fall apart when he begins showing off. Libra and Aquarius are both difficult partners for Capricorn, and she is rarely found with either of them.

AQUARIUS

A female Aquarius is very different from her male counterparts. She is calm and keeps a cool head, but she is also affectionate and open. She values loyalty above all else, and is unlikely to recover from any infidelity, though she will only divorce if this becomes a chronic trend, and she has truly been stabbed in the back. She is not interested in her partner's money, but rather, his professional success. She is unobtrusive and trusting, and will refrain from listening in on her partner's phone conversations or hacking into his email. With rare exceptions, Aquarian women make terrible housewives. But they are excellent partners in life – they are faithful, never boring, and will not reject a man, even in the most difficult circumstances. Most Aquarians are highly intuitive, and can easily tell the truth from a lie. They themselves only lie in extreme situations, which call for a "white lie" in order to avoid hurting someone's feelings.

Aquarius gets along well with Aries, Gemini, and Libra. She can also have a good relationship with a Sagittarius. Taurus often makes a successful match, though they are emotionally very different; the same goes for Virgo. Aquarius and Scorpio, Capricorn, or Cancer is a difficult match. Pisces can make a good partner as well, as both signs complement each other. Any relationship with a Leo will be tumultuous, but lasting, as Leo is selfish, and Aquarius will therefore have to be very forgiving.

PISCES

Pisces women are very adaptable, musically inclined, and erotic. They possess an innate earthly wisdom, and a good business sense. Pisces often reinvent themselves; they can be emotional, soft, and obstinate, as well as sentimental, at times. Their behavioral changes can be explained by frequent ups and downs. Pisces is charming, caring, and her outward malleability is very attractive to men. She is capable of loving selflessly, as long as the man has something to love. Even if he doesn't, she will try and take care of him until the very end. Pisces' greatest fear is poverty. They are intuitive, vulnerable, and always try to avoid conflict. They love to embellish the truth, and sometimes alcohol helps with this. Rarely, one finds extremely unbalanced, neurotic and dishonest Pisces, who are capable of turning their loved ones' lives into a living Hell!

Taurus, Capricorn, Cancer, and Scorpio make the best matches. She will be greatly attracted to a Virgo, but a lasting relationship is only likely if both partners are highly spiritual. Any union with a Libra is likely to be difficult and full of conflict. Pisces finds Gemini attractive, and they may have a very lively relationship – for a while. Occasionally, Pisces ends up with a Sagittarius, but she will have to fade into the background and entirely submit to him. If she ends up with an Aquarius, expect strong emotional outbursts, and a marriage that revolves around the need to raise their children.

Tatiana Borsch

Printed in Great Britain
by Amazon